PRAISE FOR CONSCIOUS CLASSROOM MANAGEMENT

"Every principal is going to want their staff to have access to this book . . . Rubrics for lining up, sitting down, cleaning the room - what an amazingly simple concept that makes every day activities easy to manage and very clear to all students!"

Candy Plahy
Director of Beginning
Teacher Programs (BTSA)
Placentia Yorba Linda, CA

"This is a book for everyone - for classroom teachers and beginning teachers; for principals who wish to coach their teachers to more effective ways of facilitating learning; and for teacher preparation instructors who can use the text to spark meaningful dialogue about teaching, students, and the management of learning. Written in a wonderfully conversational style, it's almost like Rick is having a one-on-one talk with you about your work!"

Mike Murphy
Director of Programs
National Staff
Development Council

i

"Rick's focus on 'prevention before intervention' is right on. His proactive strategies help teachers reduce stress, while dramatically decreasing the time and energy they spend on managing their classes."

Denise Leonard
Coordinator of
New Teacher Programs (BTSA)
Torrance, CA

"The strategies that Rick shares have made a world of difference in my classroom. I've read quite a few books on classroom management, but none compare to this book's strategies. It's a must read for new teachers!"

Nina Osberg
1st year teacher, 2nd grade
Tacoma, WA

"Conscious Classroom Management details the thought processes that are critical to effective teaching. It clearly spells out the how and why with specific strategies for success. A great book that should be a must-read for all teachers."

Rick Morris
Education Consultant
Creator of
New Management

"Written in an easy, conversational manner, rich with humor, Rick Smith's book not only tells us what to do Monday, but also reminds us why we entered the teaching profession in the first place. It shows us both the nuts and bolts of classroom management – and the heart. I would recommend it to the beginning teachers with whom I work, and also to those with a lifetime of experience in teaching."

Martha Allen
*High School English Teacher
and Mentor*
Marin County, CA
Teacher of the Year

"Finally! Conscious Classroom Management is sure to be a welcome relief to new and veteran teachers struggling with management issues. This easy-to-use book shifts the focus of classroom management from the suppression of certain behaviors to the cultivation of others. Aligned with the principles of positive youth development, this guide can shift both teacher and student perspectives about what their roles are in classrooms."

Susan Verducci, Ph.D
Center on Adolescence
Stanford University

Conscious Classroom Management:
UNLOCKING THE SECRETS OF GREAT TEACHING
By Rick Smith

Published by Conscious Teaching Publications
21 Crest Road
Fairfax, California 94930
Phone: 800-667-6062
Email: ricksmith@consciousteaching.com
Website: www.consciousteaching.com

I.S.B.N. 978-0-9796355-0-2 Library of Congress card number pending

Cover Design and Cartoons: Tom Hermansen
Book Design: Mary Lambert
Printed in Canada

Conscious Classroom Management:

UNLOCKING THE SECRETS OF GREAT TEACHING

Rick Smith

Illustrations by Tom Hermansen

CONSCIOUS TEACHING PUBLICATIONS
SAN RAFAEL, CA

TABLE OF CONTENTS

Foreword xi

Acknowledgements xiv

1. Introduction 2
   How to Use This Book 6

Foundation – Who We Are 9

2. Assume the Best 10
   Teachers Teach Procedures and Behavior 11
   Students Want to Learn Content 13
   Students Want to Learn Behavior 13
   Phil the Baiter 16

3. Inner Authority 20
   The Inner Authority Continuum 21
   When and How to Apologize 23
   Growing in Inner Authority 26
   Approaches that work 26

4. Ask for Help 30
   Characteristics of a Good Teacher 32
   Countering Isolation 34
   My bumpy start 35
   Synonyms for help 36
   We receive the help we ask for 37
   Openness is win-win 37
   Strategies 38
   Help-ful tips for new teachers 38
   Giving students chances to ask for help 40
   Remembering we are role models 41

> Checkout
> "What To Do First?"
> on page 131 if you
> are pressed for time.

5. Got Stress? 42
   The Biggest Source of Teacher Stress 43
   Our Infinite Job Description 45
   Find What Works 46
     Five minutes a day 47
   Taking Care of Ourselves. 48
     The bottom line of expectations. 50
     Stress before the December holidays 51

Prevention – What We Do Proactively .. 53

6. Holding Our Ground 54
   The Firm and Soft Paradox 56
   Saying "No" 57
   Don't Over-explain 57
   Characteristics of an Effective "No" 59
   Ambiguous Characteristics of "No" 60
   Anger vs. Reactivity. 60

7. Positive Connections. 64
   The Ingredients — Caring 65
     Doing what's best, not what's easiest 66
     Head, heart, and gut 67
   The Recipe — Strategies 69
     Choices 69
     Specific things we can do 69
     Writing vs. speaking. 73
   Avoiding Pitfalls. 73
     Getting too personal 73
     Prepare for the worst — assume the best 75
     We are the boss. Period. 76
     There will be times when we are not liked — hated, even. . 76
     The emotional charge-transfer game 78
     Classes have no memory (though kids do) 79

8. Teaching Procedures 80
   Procedures Are the Railroad Tracks — Content Is the Train. . 82
   What Procedures Do We Need? 83
   How Do I Teach Procedures? 85
      1. Practicing procedures: group work 86
      2. Reviewing procedures regularly 88
      3. Two procedures per lesson 90
      4. Rubrics for procedures 92
   Things to Do 93
      Getting the class quiet 93
      Directions, questions 100

9. Consistency 104
   1. Hand and Mouth Dis-ease 106
   2. Arguing With the Ref 108
   3. The Popcorn Effect 110
   Other Consistency Keys 112

10. Getting Ready 114
   What to Do Before School Starts 115
   Before-School Checklist 116
      Feeling overwhelmed? 123
      What if you're hired at the last minute? 124
      Room arrangement 125
   Starting School 127
      Activities for the first few days 127
   What to Do First? 131
      Before the first day 131
      Procedures 132
      Behavior 133
      Content 133

11. Lesson Design. 134
  The Big Picture. 135
    The five-step lesson plan 136
    Designing lessons. 138
  Starting the Lesson 138
    Strategies 138
  The Lesson Itself. 146
    Strategies 146
    Including all students. 155
    Movement breaks 155
  Closure. 157
    Strategies 157

Intervention – What We Do in Response . . 161

12. Rules and Consequences. 162
  Principles. 164
  Rules 165
    Strategies 165
  Consequences – Five Key Assumptions 167
    Dan and the flying hammer. 168
  The Nuts and Bolts of Consequences. 172
    Part 1. Which consequences to choose 172
    Part 2. Implementing consequences 182
    Part 3. Documenting misbehavior 191
    Part 4. Making changes in our system 193
    Part 5. Extrinsic vs. intrinsic rewards 196

13. Breaking the Cycle of Student Misbehavior . 200
  Assumptions That Make a Difference 201
    Addressing the causes 201
    Why students act out 202
    Helpful approaches 203

Five Keys for Permanent Change. 204
Example 1. Elementary school 205
Example 2. Middle school 207
Example 3. High school 208
Tips for Temporary Change. 210
Strategies 210

14. Putting It All Together – Final Thoughts . . . 214
Classroom Management: The Big Picture 215
An observation checklist 216
Teaching and Learning: The Big Picture. 219
A recipe for learning 219
Our Own Lives: The Really Big Picture. 221

Index. 226

About the Author 240

FOREWORD

How can we get students to reach standards, while struggling with many unmotivated students who refuse to engage in our lessons? Rick Smith's new book offers answers. Practical, teacher-friendly, and easy-to-read, Conscious Classroom Management provides realistic, research-supported suggestions for effectively managing a classroom. This book is filled with a wealth of powerful tools for teachers to use immediately and a perspective that leads to more productive classrooms over time. The depth of Rick's offerings to educators comes from his years in the field. He has drawn from his extensive experience teaching at-risk students and coaching new and veteran teachers, to come up with a winner.

"Give a man a fish and he eats for a day. Teach him to fish and he eats for a lifetime." Teachers are so in need of "stuff they can use" – of nourishment, that sometimes if we try to teach them to fish, they will starve to death. They need a combination of ideas and strategies they can use immediately, along with the foundation and understanding that allows them to develop far beyond mere survival in the classroom. This book provides both. Beginning and struggling teachers desperate for ideas for Monday, and accomplished teachers, looking for a deeper appreciation of their craft, have a book that effectively addresses the how and the why of effective classroom management.

Rick's book takes a magnifying glass to great teaching, revealing the key assumptions that allow teachers to organize their teaching and discipline students in ways that invite student cooperation.

Throughout his book is an underlying focus on bringing out the best in students and in teachers. What a concept that teaching is win-win! That teachers teach behavior, and students are here to learn it. That classroom structure is a tool for learning. That students need and want to learn behavior as well as content. And that procedures are the railroad tracks that allow the train of content to move unimpeded by student misbehaviors.

Many teachers have a common experience: they go into a classroom, do exactly what they are "supposed to do," mimic their master teachers, and yet their classrooms are rife with unwanted chaos. Why? What undermines their success, and what can they do about it? Many of the answers are in this book. It addresses the nitty gritty, offering hundreds of tools and tips. It also reveals the invisible element of teacher inner authority, showing how critical it is for success, and offering specific and practical ways teachers can exercise their "muscle" of inner authority.

In many cases, teachers' feelings and assumptions are the driving force behind what they do and how they do it. Unlike most other books on teaching, Conscious Classroom Management: Unlocking the Secrets of Great Teaching addresses these anxieties, hopes, and concerns, to get at the heart of how teachers can not only manage classes successfully, but also enjoy themselves and their students in the process. It addresses the human elements of teaching, and provides a lens that allows for forgiveness, relaxation, and inspiration while the job gets done. It is a rich delightful mixture of stories, humor, strategies, and insights into what works in the classroom. You can flip to just about any page and walk away with things to implement and things to ponder. Or you can read it from cover to cover, receiving the deeper understanding of what our role is and how we can best nurture ourselves and our students.

I met Rick several years ago at a national education conference. We hit it off immediately, sharing stories and strategies for making a difference for teachers and their students. Since then he has reached tens of thousands of teachers and hundreds of thousands of students, sharing his simple yet powerful strategies for classroom management and motivation.

In my work with teachers, schools, and districts across the country on effectively improving teaching to increase achievement for all students, I am asked to recommend immediately usable resources to help teachers with classroom management. With *Conscious Classroom Management: Unlocking the Secrets of Great Teaching*, everyone can discover how to make an even greater difference for kids, manage classes more effectively, and enjoy teaching more.

Spence Rogers, *Founder and Director*
PEAK LEARNING SYSTEMS
Author of:
    The High Performance Toolbox
    Motivation & Learning
    Teaching Tips
    Teaching Treasures
    Teaching and Training Techniques
    Teaching for Excellence

ACKNOWLEDGEMENTS

First and foremost, I wish to thank my students, who first drove me crazy, and then drove me sane.

My first years as a teacher were rough, challenging, and ultimately wonderful. Much of what I learned as a foundation for this book came through trial and error, and the patient guidance of some very wise people.

I wish to thank Mary Lambert and Barry Tellman who, during those first years, taught me to look in the mirror when things weren't going well, assume the best about myself and my students, and get "back in the saddle."

In addition, I want to acknowledge my mentors – Cynthia Brown, Marny Sorgen, and Carole Tateishi, who held my hand while kicking me in the butt, all the while modeling effective mentoring.

Putting together a book like this is no easy task. It is consuming, sometimes maddening, and consistently humbling. My respect for book writers has soared, as has my gratitude for those who supported me through the process, either logistically or emotionally. At the risk of leaving out scores of people who have supported me, I will mention a few.

For his dedication and creativity, I wish to thank Tom Hermansen. For sharing with me her love affair with words, and for her tireless cheerleading, I wish to thank Kristin Donnan. And for overall support through every phase of the book, I wish to thank Mary Lambert.

Others offering needed emotional support, advice for me as a teacher-trainer over the years, and/or help with the crafting and birthing of this book, often to the tune of many hours, include:

Rick Curwin, Jeffrey Smith, Mike Murphy, Susan Verducci, Martha Allen, Rick Morris, Michael Zipkin, Mary Waetjen, Venus Elyse, Nancy Tarascio, Mort Smith, Robynn Smith, Daniela de Vasques, James Schlesselman, Dave Nidorf, My dear friends at KIMYA, Arnie Riesen, Pat Wolfe, Kathy Perez, Esther Wright, Spence Rogers, Rich Allen, Cindy Douglas, and Claire Paul.

1

INTRODUCTION

> "I'm a teacher. A teacher is someone who leads. There is no magic here. I do not walk on water. I do not part the sea. I just love children."
>
> — MARVA COLLINS

ON MY FIRST DAY as a student teacher, I was sent to observe how an effective teacher set up his classroom management system. The theory: I would reproduce the successful system six months later when I took over my first classes for student teaching. It was a great idea.

It failed miserably.

Enthusiastic in my ignorance, I entered the classroom of a veteran tenth-grade English teacher, my eyes open for every detail, my pen in hand. I was ready to learn. Throughout the course of the first week, I noticed that Mr. Miller's classes ran incredibly smoothly. When he said to his students, "Open your books to page 27," every book opened to page 27. The students were silent, leaning forward, attentive. I saw no evidence of hard-hitting management strategies or overbearing lists of rules. I saw *nothing*. My notebook was empty. I thought to myself, "This is easy. I just say it, and they do it..."

Visions of students lining up behind me, the model teacher, appeared in my mind's eye. I could just see it; these kids would happily follow my lead as I journeyed into the wonders of learn-

I thought to myself, "This is easy. I just say it, and they do it..."

ing. My classes would be even better than Mr. Miller's; they would break the mold. I would have no need for discipline because my students would tap into their natural hunger to learn. I would be their relaxed, loving, and skillful guide, seamlessly employing invisible management strategies.

I came to earth later that same first week while observing another tenth-grade English teacher attempting the same lesson Mr. Miller had taught. When this ineffective teacher asked the students to open their books to page 27, several students did indeed open their books. Some were on the right page. Some even had the correct book. But this simple task was torturous. Amid an outpouring of chatter, complaints, confusion, and paper airplanes, any sense of order within the room simply disappeared.

At first glance, I couldn't figure out why Mr. Miller had been so much more effective. Since I definitely didn't want a career in dodging paper airplanes, I made it my mission to break the code. I began with a basic question, "Why can the same request asked of two groups of students result in opposite behaviors?"

The answer to this — and a million questions like it — is the motivation behind my writing this book.

Effective classroom management is essentially invisible.

It is so seamless that unless we know what to look for, we won't be able to see it. Hundreds of thousands of student teachers, new teachers, and even veteran teachers each year have this same experience: they look for effective classroom management strategies in their classroom observations, but:

▲ They don't know what to look for
▲ They don't see anything
▲ If they do see something, they don't know how to translate it into their own classroom teaching

As a new teacher, I became obsessed with understanding invisible management. I was desperate to survive in my classes, and asked, begged, pleaded with, interrogated anyone I knew who might be able to help me. Still, my first years were a struggle. Later, as a mentor teacher working closely with new teachers, my obsession remained — but in a slightly different form. Simply growing into a more effective teacher was not enough; I also wanted to find a way to make the invisible visible to others. I wanted to communicate to other teachers how to "see" classroom management and how to translate it into their teaching. To do this, I sought to make effective classroom management tangible by moving it out of the realm of "instinct."

A Closer Look

By slowing down the camera — by looking more closely at what is happening both in the classroom and behind the scenes — we can increase our awareness of what works and why, thus providing a road map for improving our classroom experience.

This book describes the key elements I have discovered along the way that help create classroom management conscious. By slowing down the camera — by looking more closely at what is happening both in the classroom and behind the scenes — we can increase our awareness of what works and why, thus providing a road map for improving our classroom experience.

Throughout the book, I refer to a fictional teacher named Mrs. Allgood. Like the effective tenth-grade English teacher I observed my first week in the profession, she has fabulous classroom management skills. Looking closely at both what she does and the thinking behind what she does can shed light on essential skills for managing the classroom. Imagine that she teaches your grade and subject area(s), and is just down the hall.

I also refer to a not-so-effective teacher named Mrs. Meanswell. She tries hard but is struggling. So far, Mrs. Meanswell cannot consistently make cause-and-effect connections between her management choices and her classes' behavior patterns.

Mrs. Meanswell is not necessarily a new teacher, nor is Mrs. Allgood necessarily a veteran. Teachers of all levels of experience have all levels of effectiveness in the classroom. Further, all of us have "Allgood moments" as well as "Meanswell moments." Even though Mrs. Allgood represents an ideal to strive for, even she has "Meanswell-like moments." There is no perfect model teacher; regardless of our levels of skill, we are constantly learning.

Throughout the book I use quotes with various icons to emphasize certain ideas. Though there is some overlap, in general the magnifying glass indicates an idea that is often invisible, the apple icon focuses on global ideas, summaries and advice, and the Mrs. Allgood icon is about teacher-to-teacher insights and practical suggestions.

When referring to a typical student who acts out, I often use the name "Mark." This is because challenging students inevitably make a "mark" in our awareness. In cases where I refer to teachers or students other than by name, I refer to teachers in the feminine gender and students in the masculine. This is done simply to help with clarity, and is not intended to make any political or pedagogical statements.

How to Use This Book

This book is for any K-12 teacher who would like to improve his or her classroom management skills. There are many references in the book to new teachers, yet this information will work for teachers of all levels of experience. It is also for mentor teachers who are focused on helping other teachers improve.

Although this book is focused on practical strategies, I have included many ideas about teacher attitude and assumptions that at first might seem theoretical. This is because effective classroom management is more than just plugging in a series of consequences to match student misbehavior. It is a complex of approaches that draws on an understanding of three primary areas: the students, the teacher, and the relationship between the two. Success lies in awareness not only of our actions, but also of who we are as people. These two "prongs" form the basis for effective management:

Who We Are ⟵⟶ What We Do

Who we are refers to how we hold ourselves internally, and thus how we come across to our students. Are we rigid and reactive, focusing too much on our own performance to actually communicate with our students? Are we laid back and loose, too focused on being the students' friend to consistently teach behavior? Or are we firm and soft simultaneously, assuming both the best about our students — that they want to learn behavior, and the best about ourselves — that we are human beings who have the students' best interest in mind and heart?

What we do refers to the nuts and bolts of classroom management — specific strategies for designing and maintaining a positive classroom environment, connecting with students, and taking care of business.

The combination of who we are and what we do makes for effective classroom management. It influences the manner in which we communicate with students, parents, and administrators, and it determines our effectiveness in moments of potential conflict. How do we implement consequences? How do we hold our ground with students without being mean, without creating battles down the road?

Taken as a whole, *Conscious Classroom Management* outlines a practical guide to surviving and thriving in the classroom. The "who" of classroom management can be found in the first main section, called Foundation. "What" is divided into Prevention and Intervention. The figure on the next page represents these key elements.

When searching for hints that address one of these issues immediately, feel free to think of the table of contents as a web page: click on the most appropriate chapter, and go there directly. Each chapter is written so that generally it will stand on its own, addressing one of these critical elements of classroom management.

If you are truly pressed for time and are about to start your school year, go straight to the section called "What to do first?" on page 131. It will help guide you through your first days of school.

A Closer Look

The combination of who we are and what we do makes for effective classroom management.

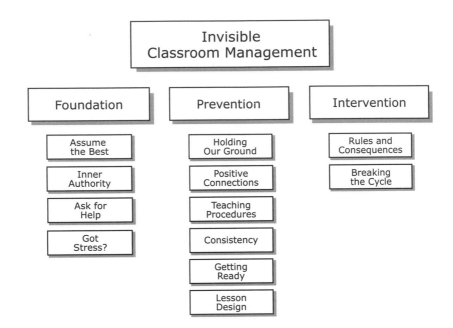

The more I explore classroom management and the more I explore myself, the more connections I make between my growth as a person and my abilities as an educator. I am forty-two years old. This book has taken me forty-two years to write. I've been a new teacher, a veteran teacher, a mentor teacher, and a teacher trainer. I've observed and coached over a hundred beginning and veteran teachers, and I am still constantly learning. I invite you to "get lost" in this book, and discover not only the quick fixes you need for your classes, but also the deeper connection you have to yourself and your students. There is no limit to the wonder to be uncovered in this exploration.

If you are truly pressed for time and are about to start your school year, go straight to the section called "What to do first?" on page 131.

FOUNDATION —
Who We Are

> *"You teach a little by what you say.*
> *You teach the most by what you are."*
>
> — DR. HENRIETTA MEARS

2

ASSUME
THE BEST

"It's not who you are that holds you back, it's who you think you're not."

— AUTHOR UNKNOWN

"Thank you, Johnny, for raising your hand." HERMANSEN

EFFECTIVE TEACHERS HAVE internalized certain key positive assumptions about their students and themselves, to the point where they aren't always aware of what those assumptions are. We need to unearth, identify, and focus on these assumptions, because they form the foundation of our entire teaching experience and frame every action we take. When we start to assume the best about our students and ourselves, teaching changes and results happen.

Teachers Teach Procedures and Behavior

We may have gotten into the teaching profession to teach science, music, or foreign language, but pretty soon we discover that, in reality, we are in the profession to teach people. And people have many needs beyond particular content areas. Therefore, we teach content, procedures necessary to facilitate learning that content, and appropriate behavior. Moreover, we shouldn't teach behavior quickly to get it out of the way in order to teach the good stuff. Behavior *is* the good stuff. Students need to learn what's appropriate, what's not appropriate, how to tell the difference, and how to discipline themselves to make nurturing choices. Life is about making choices, receiving consequences, and learning from our successes and mistakes. When we teach behavior, we are really teaching life skills.

Wise Apple Advice

When we start to assume the best about our students and ourselves, teaching changes and results happen.

It helps to imagine that the contract we sign to be a teacher doesn't just state that we will teach third grade or teach five classes of math. It also says in large, invisible-ink letters that we will teach our students appropriate behavior (some contracts actually include a statement like this).

When we assume that we are here to teach appropriate behavior, a significant change takes place. We stop and face behavior issues head on, instead of doing "drive-by discipline." Instead of a "hurry-up" attitude that actually takes more time because of the resulting chaos, students tend to "get it" the first time, and thus we have more time to focus on content. When Mrs. Allgood disciplines students, she assumes that she is here to teach behavior and that students are here to learn it. Both her verbal and nonverbal presentations naturally reflect these assumptions. She doesn't beg, advertise, or sell. She simply addresses the behavior squarely, and moves on.

Learning behavior is at least equally if not more important than learning content. When I taught in an alternative school for at-risk high school students, some of them were quite bright. I had one who could even do quadratic equations in his head, while he was behind bars. He had the smarts to do the math, but not to avoid getting in trouble with the law.

As students learn appropriate behavior, they also accumulate critical life-long skills. In his book *Emotional Intelligence*, Daniel Goleman points to several key indicators of emotional intelligence that are directly related to behavior management, among which are our ability to:

- ▲ Address anger
- ▲ Sooth ourselves
- ▲ Delay gratification

When we effectively teach behavior to our students, we enhance their ability to mature. We thus teach the whole person. Teaching behavior is not a necessary evil — it is a "necessary wonderful."

Students Want to Learn Content

Mrs. Allgood assumes that students want to learn the content she is teaching, even if they don't pay attention or if they tell her that they aren't interested. This allows her to keep looking for ways to get them interested and motivated, and for teaching strategies that make the information palatable, even exciting. If she assumes, "Since he's not interested, it doesn't matter what I do; I might as well not put any effort into it," she'll develop a cynical attitude toward her students and toward her teaching. She also won't have any fun.

> I had one student who could even do quadratic equations in his head, while he was behind bars.

A more positive assumption helps her keep her passion for the content she is teaching, and provides a better chance that her passion will rub off on her students. Chapter 11, "Lesson Design," addresses this in more detail.

Students Want to Learn Behavior

There is an invisible covenant between Mrs. Allgood and each of her students. The student's covenant says:

"Please teach me appropriate behavior in a safe and structured environment. I may act out, I may behave in ways that suggest I am not interested, but in truth I really want to learn appropriate behavior and I won't be satisfied unless you are holding your ground teaching this to me."

The teacher's covenant says:

"I will do my best to teach you appropriate behavior in a safe and structured environment. I will assume that you want to learn behavior no matter what evidence you may demonstrate to the contrary."

When Mark acts out in Mrs. Allgood's class, for example, it's often for one of two reasons:

1. He wants to let her know that he has not yet fully learned the appropriate behavior. She needs to teach it to him again, perhaps in a different way or by breaking things into smaller pieces. Maybe she needs to provide him a set of consequences or supports that will allow him to better see his options for appropriate behavior.

Helping Mark learn behavior is just like helping him learn math. If he doesn't get it, she may have to teach it more thoroughly or differently. She always points out what needs to be corrected and moves on. Whether she's teaching math or behavior, there's little or no animosity or challenge to her authority because Mark and Mrs. Allgood are on the same side. Please note: No matter how effective Mrs. Allgood is, there is no guarantee that Mark will demonstrate learned behavior. He will still make independent choices, some of which may lead to inappropriate behavior. All she can do is be consistent and thorough.

2. He is testing her. He wants to make sure that she will hold up her end of their covenant. He wants to know that the boundaries are clear and consistent, but not hard-edged or threatening. He says to himself, "Let's see if this teacher's class is safe and structured. I'm going to break a rule and see what she does."

If Mark acts out and she comes down on him like a ton of bricks, then he sees that she is not creating a safe environment. If, on the other hand, he breaks a rule and she ignores it and he gets away with it, then she is not creating a structured environment. When either of these occurs, he subconsciously tells himself,

> "I don't think the teacher understood. I'm going to assume the best about her. So I'll break another rule to give her the opportunity to come through with safety and structure."

So Mark breaks another rule. Once he sees that Mrs. Allgood won't react and blame him for testing, and that she won't ignore him and let him get away with it, he'll know that her classroom is a good place for him to learn behavior, and he'll end his test.

If the walls — the boundaries or rules of the class — are strong yet soft, then students confirm that indeed the teacher is honoring the invisible contract. Then they can focus on honoring their end of the bargain. Simply put, when students test us, they want us to pass the test.

Another way to think of this assumption is to imagine that every moment every one of our students has just asked us:

> ## "Could you please teach me how to behave? What do I need to do or know in order to best learn behavior?"

So when we ask a student to change seats or see us after school or pay attention, we are simply addressing his question, which he asked in all sincerity.

Mrs. Allgood says

When students test us, they want us to pass the test.

This assumption — regardless of whether or not it's actually true — allows us to enforce a whole range of consequences without unduly ruffling students' feathers, and without taking our rough days home with us. Students do not act out because they are trying to "get us." They are not "bad kids," intent on spreading their "badness" to their classmates:

Negative Assumption	*Positive Assumption*
▲ They are bad kids	▲ They haven't fully learned the appropriate behavior
▲ They don't want to learn	▲ They want to know that the classroom environment will be safe and structured
▲ They are trying to hurt the teacher	▲ They are signaling the teacher to teach behavior more thoroughly or differently

For a more thorough exploration of why students act out, see Chapter 13, "When Consequences Don't Work: Breaking the Cycle of Student Misbehavior."

Phil the Baiter

I was student-teaching a ninth-grade English "class-from-heck," at a high-achievement public school where a significant percentage of the students went on to college. However, in my class of twenty-seven students, nine of them, as it later turned out, would not graduate from high school on time or at all. Of course, at the time I didn't know this. All I knew was that I was having an incredibly hard time managing my class, and that I must be a terrible teacher because my students acted out so much.

Of all the tough students in that class, Phil was the toughest (I quickly got my "Phil" of his antics). He had a nasty habit of challenging everything I did. He'd often play to the crowd, saying things like, "This is pointless. Why are we doing this?!?" I would then immediately feel about two feet tall, as everyone else began to consider his question. Invariably, whenever Phil spoke in class, he would trigger the other students into contributing to complaints, chatter, and ultimately, chaos.

During most nights of that semester, when lying down to sleep, the last thought I had was of Phil pestering me. In the mornings, I would wake up and Phil's face would immediately appear in my consciousness. I tried to design all my lessons so that they would be "Phil-proof."

During most nights of that semester, when lying down to sleep, the last thought I had was of Phil pestering me. I tried to design all my lessons so that they would be "Phil proof."

Phil was a smart kid. He had a sixth sense about how to push my buttons and get me right to the edge of my tolerance before he would back down and play the role of the innocent, dutiful student. My semester with that class began in late January. Sometime in early May, I finally got up the courage to send Phil to the office. It was perhaps a combination of my increased resolve and Phil's over-confidence. One day he just went slightly too far, and I held my ground. After he left and the echo of his complaints receded, the class became very quiet. Things that day ran incredibly smoothly. This was, I believe, both because of Phil's absence and the students' understanding that I was suddenly willing to enforce consequences.

Phil returned the next day, and was somewhat better behaved. Though his behavior was never great, it clearly improved from that point on.

On the last day of the semester, I gave my students an evaluation form, in which they had the opportunity to assess my abilities as a teacher. On the last section of the evaluation there was a question that simply asked for comments. In that section, four students, independent of one another, wrote

"You should have kicked Phil out sooner."

This was a revelation to me. The first thing I did was beat myself up for several days. "Oh, I'm a terrible teacher. Oh, I didn't do it right." But after licking my wounds, I examined these comments and realized something very illuminating. Two students who wrote this were buddies of Phil's. When Phil had acted out in class, they had joined in, hanging tenaciously to his coattails. They were in essence saying to me:

"Although we won't admit it publicly, we want to learn. We don't have the self-esteem to stand up to Phil. We don't have the impulse control to discipline ourselves all the time. That's your job. We want you to hold the line and facilitate our learning."

> Content, procedures, and behavior are the functional trinity of the classroom, and students want to learn them all.

Students want to learn. They want to learn content, they want to learn the procedures and routines that allow for learning content, and they want to learn appropriate behavior. If we catch them in their more "sober" and open moments, when they are not trying to impress their peers or defend themselves, they will admit this — regardless of how old they are, what type of ethnic or family background they have, or their apparent ability or lack of ability.

When I was a new teacher, I didn't fully embrace these positive assumptions, and it caused a painful cycle. Kids would act out. I'd use this as evidence to assume that they were bad kids. They'd get the message that I didn't respect or really see them, so they'd act out some more, reinforcing my negative assumptions. Making the choice to assume the best about them, even as they acted out, helped save my sanity many times.

Wise Apple Advice

Assumptions – the Abridged Version

The bottom line on assumptions? Assume the best, be on the same side as our students, know that they want and need to learn behavior, treat ourselves and our students with respect and dignity, take deep breaths, and know that in the long run we will land on our feet.

3

INNER
AUTHORITY

> *"Education is the ability to listen to almost anything without losing your temper or your self-confidence."*
>
> — ROBERT FROST

The Inner Authority Continuum

WE ARE AUTHORS of what happens in the classroom. In order to write a successful script — to make our classroom environment smooth and harmonious — we must marshal our inner resources and consciously direct it. Developing our "inner authority" can make all the difference in being an effective teacher. Inner authority doesn't involve holding our breath or gearing up for battle or carrying ourselves in an aggressive way. It is a relaxed, natural state that permeates everything we do, in the classroom and elsewhere.

Our inner authority affects how we give directions, pass out papers, talk with kids one-on-one. It provides the foundation for our job satisfaction, our peace of mind, everything.

I once mentored a new P.E. teacher at a middle school. He was confused because none of the other P.E. teachers ever used consequences, yet their classes ran smoothly. If he didn't use consequences, his students acted out like crazy. The difference: the other teachers had spent several years relying on consequences, until such time that they had internalized a no-nonsense firm and soft quality in their voices and postures. Their students knew that acting out was not in their best interest; these teachers had already passed their "tests." While veteran teachers are not necessarily better managers, in this case they were; they had learned from the trials that the new guy was just beginning to face.

A Closer Look

Our inner authority affects how we give directions, pass out papers, talk with kids one-on-one. It provides the foundation for our job satisfaction, our peace of mind, everything.

Situations like the P.E. dilemma might seem to be more "obviously" or "visibly" related to actions — "acting out leads to consequences." However, the "invisible" truth lies in the teacher's inner authority; something seemingly nebulous that can drive novices like Mrs. Meanswell nuts. In fact, even many relatively effective Mrs. Allgoods don't know how they do it or how to explain it. A typical conversation about this might be:

Mrs. Meanswell: One of my students is constantly disrupting my class. What would you do in this situation?

Mrs. Allgood: Well, my students know that I will just not tolerate that kind of behavior.

Mrs. Meanswell, who means well, studiously takes notes from Mrs. Allgood, writing, "I will not tolerate that behavior..." Of course, that kind of advice doesn't really have a whole lot of benefit. What Mrs. Allgood is really referring to is her place on the continuum of inner authority. It's an invisible thing, but boy, does it make a difference.

Inner Apology ←——→ Inner Authority

The polar opposite of inner authority is inner apology, and it is deadly in the classroom. We can never have too much inner authority, because it facilitates calm and harmony, and imparts to the students a sense that their ship is being steered by capable hands. Inner apology, on the other hand, preys on our insecurities. It reflects a sense that our authority is questionable, and that we are unsure of our decisions. It imparts an essence of our apologizing for being in charge. This can happen to the most effective teachers. Even Mrs. Allgood, who is seemingly in gracious command of her classroom, might stumble on her relatively advanced march along the continuum, given the right set of circumstances. For example, when a secondary teacher teaches the same new and risky lesson to three classes in a row, the first time is often filled with misgiving, question, confusion, and an undermining dynamic of apology. But by the third class, the teacher has it down and is clear and firm and right on track.

— Wise Apple Advice

> We can never have too much inner authority, because it facilitates calm and harmony, and imparts to the students a sense that their ship is being steered by capable hands.

When and How to Apologize

Many teachers believe that to steer their ships effectively, they cannot appear to waver, and certainly they cannot apologize. This is both true and not true. Sometimes it is okay, even essential, that teachers apologize to students. Mrs. Allgood has learned to do it without losing control of the rudder; her inner authority comes to her rescue.

When we "blow it" in front of the class and humiliate a student, it's okay to apologize to that student in front of the whole class. Public humiliation outweighs a private apology. This can be in the form of apologizing to both him and to the class for our behavior, or apologizing to him in front of the class. Similarly, if we "lose it" with the whole class, it is often appropriate to apologize later in front of the whole class.

There are two diametrically opposed ways to apologize, as outlined in the chart below. When Mrs. Allgood apologizes, she is taking the heat, and not apologizing for the fact that she's apologizing. Mrs. Meanswell, though perhaps using the same words as Mrs. Allgood, is trying to deflect the heat, and is apologizing inside — undermining herself — as she apologizes to the class.

Mrs. Meanswell	Mrs. Allgood
▲ Does apologize internally	▲ Doesn't apologize internally
▲ Looks away	▲ Faces the students
▲ Her statements sound like questions ("Yesterday, I kind of blew it? I'm sorry? Okay?")	▲ Makes statements ("Yesterday, I blew it. I am so sorry.")
▲ Is jumpy	▲ Is grounded
▲ Bobs and weaves, and/or backs away from students as she talks	▲ Stands firm and/or moves slowly toward students as she talks
▲ Blames (either herself or the kids)	▲ Takes responsibility
▲ Self-effacing	▲ Self-affirming
▲ Deflects the heat	▲ Takes the heat
▲ Speaks what she thinks the kids want to hear	▲ Speaks what she knows
▲ Performs her feelings	▲ Expresses her feelings
▲ Is questionably sincere, and is somewhat mechanical in her apology	▲ Is clearly sincere, and feels empathy for what she put the students through
▲ Her apology questions her caring	▲ Her apology affirms her caring

The difference in quality between the two apologies is imme-diately obvious. There's a weight, a presence, and a silence that permeates Mrs. Allgood's apology, resulting in a more silent and thoughtful response from the students. In Mrs. Meanswell's case, the students get uncomfortable and squirmy as a reflection of her own discomfort and squirminess.

As a teacher, when I gave a "Meanswell-like" apology, the kids would often respond by acting out even more. Kids would some-times call out, "You should be sorry! You did blow it!" I'd leave class that day thinking that my students were just mean kids. If, however, my apology was a genuine act of self-forgiveness, the kids would be right with me. On occasion, I actually received applause from the students when I apologized, during which I thought to myself, "I've got to blow it with these kids more often..." This makes sense. If José comes to school the day after I've blown up at the class, he may well be feeling incredibly resistant, powerless, and angry at having to face me again. If I apologize sincerely in a way that he knows I mean it, it gives him a chance to exhale. The chip that has been lodged on his shoulder for the past twenty-four hours has a chance to dissolve.

If we are going to apologize to our students, let's not do it unless we're actually sorry. Students of all ages and abilities can sniff out insincerity a mile away. Also, let's try not to beat our-selves up when we apologize. Let's simply state the obvious, take responsibility, own it, and let it go.

The choice of whether to apologize internally is at the essence of Conscious Classroom Management. Apologizing internally for the fact that we are apologizing comes across like a "drive-by apol-ogy." We are never fully facing the students. We are pushing away the "charge" of the situation. That charge is twofold. First, we are literally in charge, in the sense that we are the authority figure in the classroom. Second, there's an emotional charge associated with apologizing to our students.

If we are not embracing the fact that we are literally in charge, incoherence will build inside us—we are in fact in charge, yet we are still apologizing for it. This will tend to be reflected in incoherent student behavior in the classroom. We need to coherently hold our ground with the noise in our head that says that we should apologize for the fact that we're in charge. As we do this, we'll be able to more readily hold our ground with our students. Emotionally, if we think that good teachers never make mistakes, we are setting ourselves up for a fall. Inevitably, we will make mistakes, and with the wrong mindset we'll tend to give self-effacing "Meanswell-like" apologies. Further, we'll be leaning in the direction of self-effacing communication (teaching on thin-ice) to some extent all the time in the classroom, in anticipation of future mistakes that we are trying to avoid.

Mrs. Allgood says

Apologizing internally for the fact that we are apologizing comes across like a "drive-by apology."

What if the kids' poor behavior triggered our poor behavior? In this case, we can unilaterally apologize for our response, offering no excuses and pointing no causal fingers. Subsequently, perhaps quite soon after, we can let the students know that their behavior was inappropriate. But if we mix these two, and blame their behavior for our explosion, our apology isn't clear, we're not taking responsibility, and worst of all, that classroom community "exhale" that we are hoping for won't take place.

Growing in Inner Authority

Approaches that work

How do we exercise the muscle of inner authority so that we can grow along this continuum, away from inner apology? There are several keys that can help, and they are sprinkled throughout this book. Each is described below in brief, and then is covered in detail in its corresponding chapter.

Assume the best

If I assume that Mark wants to learn behavior, then when I discipline him, I assume that he wants to hear what I say, and therefore I automatically gain a certain level of self-confidence. If, on the other hand, I assume that Mark doesn't want to hear what I'm saying and will fight me, then whatever lack of self-confidence I have will rise to the surface. *(See Chapter 2).*

Ask for help

The more willing we are to be human and to ask for help, the more resilient and flexible we'll be, and the more likely we'll land on our feet in times when our inner authority is challenged. *(See Chapter 4).*

Stress

As we reduce our stress, our level of calm increases, as do our presence, our resilience, and our confidence. *(See Chapter 5).*

Holding our ground — experience

Simply by gaining teaching experience, our ability to hold our ground in difficult moments will improve. The more opportunities we have to hold our ground with students, the more we will tend to grow. This is why parents who come into the teaching profession have, I believe, a slight advantage. They've had thousands of opportunities to hold their ground with their own kids, thus exercising their muscle of inner authority. This doesn't mean that parents are necessarily better classroom managers. It just means that they've had practice. *(See Chapter 6).*

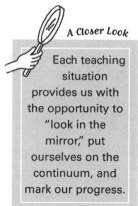

A Closer Look

Each teaching situation provides us with the opportunity to "look in the mirror," put ourselves on the continuum, and mark our progress.

Holding our ground — reflection

Each teaching situation provides us with the opportunity to "look in the mirror," put ourselves on the continuum, and mark our progress. After a particularly good or rough experience, we can ask ourselves, "Where was I apologizing for being in charge? Where was I holding my ground with the noise inside my head that said I shouldn't be making the decisions in the class? Where was I holding my ground with my arguing students — the noise outside my head?" By reflecting, we naturally speed up the growth process that comes from experience.

Practicing/role playing in front of the mirror or with a colleague or mentor teacher can also be helpful. Just as with students, our growth accelerates as we consciously practice what we are learning. *(See Chapter 6).*

Teaching procedures

This is probably the number one way teachers can exercise the muscle of inner authority. Students want to succeed, and procedures are the road map to get them there. The more specific and thorough we are in teaching and re-teaching procedures, the more our students will follow our lead, and the more we'll grow. *(See Chapter 8).*

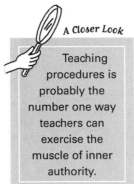

A Closer Look

Teaching procedures is probably the number one way teachers can exercise the muscle of inner authority.

Consistency

The muscle of consistency works together with the muscle of inner authority. Being consistent means holding our ground with all the distractions, sidebars, and interruptions the students can muster. As we remain focused on keeping students focused, we sharpen our skills and grow along the continuum. *(See Chapter 9).*

Getting ready

There's nothing like being prepared and organized to boost one's confidence. It can pay big dividends to be thorough in designing lessons, and to anticipate student questions and concerns before they arise. *(See Chapter 10)*.

Consequences

Students often react when they receive consequences. If we can hold our ground in a firm and soft way when they do, our presence will tend to strengthen and they'll tend to react less. *(See Chapter 12)*.

Consequences — calling parents or guardians

I once gave a "homework suggestion" to one of my beginning teachers that he call five parents a night for three straight weeks. If the kids were doing well, I suggested that he call their parents anyway. Not only did this help motivate his students, it also helped him exercise his muscle of inner authority, because he was consciously and consistently focusing on student behavior, and he was practicing being in charge. Calling parents helps exercise our muscle of inner authority because we get to practice being in charge *(see Chapter 12)*.

Mrs. Allgood says

Calling parents helps exercise our muscle of inner authority because we get to practice being in charge.

Wise Apple Advice

It's worth it

Exercising the muscle of inner authority can seem both daunting and nebulous at first. Just about all teachers seem to go through a "trial by fire" where the learning curve is steep. But over time, if we continue to practice being firm with our students without reacting, while paying attention to the other elements outlined above, we will see benefits. It's definitely worth the effort.

ASK
FOR HELP

"All learning begins with the simple phrase, 'I don't know.'"

— AUTHOR UNKNOWN
(I DON'T KNOW)

M RS. MEANSWELL IS SO SINCERE in her desire to do well that she sometimes forgets that doing well includes having bad days. She sometimes tenses up in class, trying too hard to be the perfect teacher. The result is that both she and her students need to go home and recover.

Just like everyone else, teachers make mistakes. If we walk around denying or ignoring this, not only do we set an impossible standard for ourselves, but also our students will think we expect them to be perfect. Such a set-up creates a tense and rigid environment, with students ultimately acting hard towards us as we act hard within ourselves.

If, however, we allow ourselves the "room" to be people who have feelings and imperfections, while still keeping focused on our goals as professionals, our students will receive the message that it's okay to take risks, explore, and make mistakes in the classroom. They will consequently learn more, and the classroom will have a much better chance of becoming a vibrant nurturing community.

Mrs. Allgood says

Our openness lets our students know that it's okay to take risks, explore, and make mistakes in the classroom.

If we forgive ourselves our imperfections, ultimately our students will forgive us as well — at least when they are in the classroom. They will act soft (forgiving) towards us, reflecting our own inner softness. This will have an immediate impact on our classroom management success. As our students soften, they will be more likely to behave better and follow our directions, and less likely to act out and argue. In classroom management, who we are counts equally as much as what we do.

Openness is the key to letting go of seeking unattainable perfection. It is the single-most important quality of any teacher — especially any new teacher — and most mentor teachers, support providers, and coaches would agree. For teachers to explore, take risks, and learn in the classroom, sometimes they need input from others. Knowing when our own resources need a boost is the first step. Being open to receiving that boost is the second.

Mrs. Allgood has a way of giving and receiving advice and suggestions that appears seamless. It's part of who she is to be open with her colleagues, even laughing at her mistakes while simultaneously feeling confident in her abilities. If we don't look closely, we might assume that she has never needed help and support from colleagues. But if we seek out and ask the Mrs. Allgoods in our schools, we'll discover that their openness and willingness to seek support are fundamental building blocks of that confident persona.

Characteristics of a Good Teacher

In my workshops I often run an activity where participants brainstorm characteristics of a good teacher. Many participants remember the Mrs. Allgoods who once taught them when they were students, or who currently teach across the hall. All sorts of adjectives are thrown about. A typical workshop might yield the following good teacher characteristics:

Flexible
Organized
Knowledgeable
Sense of humor
Fair
Patient
Caring
Good communicator
Reflective
Firm
Positive
Consistent
Enthusiastic
Honest

Wise Apple Advice

If we forgive ourselves our imperfections, ultimately our students will forgive us as well — at least when they are in the classroom.

After this brainstorm, I then include characteristics that I suggest are equally essential. These include:

Sometimes makes mistakes
Sometimes has bad days
Sometimes feels helpless
Sometimes feels overwhelmed
Sometimes feels stressed
Sometimes feels under-appreciated

Many of us go into the profession thinking that we are supposed to be perfect. We think we're never supposed to feel certain feelings or have certain experiences. But the reality is that we have all sorts of experiences in the classroom. We have days where we just don't want to get out of bed. We have times when we're really angry at our students.

If we don't allow for and welcome these feelings up front, then when they inevitably occur, we will do our best to try to hide or deny them. We will become rigid, and eventually tend to try to blame our students, our situations, or ourselves for why we feel the way we do. At the very least, we will tend to shy away from other teachers, because we won't want to be seen as less than stellar. Wrong move. When we "hit the wall" is precisely the time to reach out to our colleagues. Bad days are a signal, a special code other teachers know all too well, that lets us know it's a key time to talk with a colleague about how we are feeling and what is happening in our classes.

I've mentored many new teachers over the years, and just like me, all of them — beginners to veterans — sooner or later have had the experience of feeling inferior as teachers. They were not inferior. They just had that experience. But some chose to run from it. They did this by putting up walls between themselves and the students, and between themselves and me. They decided to go into "self-protection mode" and "ride out the storm." Of course, the "storm" was just life, and their decision to ride it out by retreating into their shell was what caused or magnified most of their anxiety.

Mrs. Allgood says

> When we "hit the wall" is precisely the time to reach out to our colleagues.

Countering Isolation

Let's look at the italicized list above, and focus more closely on the teacher quality "sometimes feels helpless." As a teacher, this simply means, "doesn't always know what to do." Let's say Mrs. Meanswell is in the staff room between lessons or classes. She's got fifteen minutes before she goes back to class, and she realizes that her lesson plan is not going to work. For whatever reason, what looked good last night is now clearly a bomb waiting to go off. There's another teacher in the staff room who may just be able to help. Mrs. Meanswell basically has three choices.

▲ She can apologize internally for the fact that she's not quite sure what to do, and do the "duck and cover" routine by avoiding that teacher and keeping to herself.

- ▲ She can apologize internally for the fact that she's not quite sure what to do, and put on a false bravado by pretending that everything is "great!"
- ▲ She can choose not to apologize internally for the fact that she's not quite sure what to do, and simply ask for help.

This last option can be a lifesaver. We need to find people whose opinions we trust, and then ask away without holding back, talking with mentor teachers, master teachers, supervisors, peer coaches, colleagues, foremen, whatever name our fellow teachers go by.

There's no way we can be expected to know what to do in every situation. There's no way we can do it all, know it all, make all the right decisions. We need help! This is true for all teachers, regardless of their level of experience.

My bumpy start

When I was a student teacher, I was working in a county that had a glut of teachers and very few available teaching jobs. I spent my four months of student-teaching focused not on improving my craft as a teacher, not on learning the mechanics and subtleties of the art of teaching, not on cementing relationships with mentors, but on *getting a job*. I walked around for four months trying to prove to everyone that I was the right man for the job. I focused on my mantra: "I know what to do, thank you very much, and any staff would be proud to have me as their colleague." When April/May rolled around and it became apparent to me that my classroom management system had huge holes in it, I had a very bumpy time getting help because I had isolated myself from my much more experienced colleagues.

Conversely, one of my student-teacher friends at the time had a similar assignment at a similar school. Sometime in the first week of her student teaching, she fell apart crying, asking some of the staff members of her department for help. The next day when she came back to school, in her mailbox were lesson plans, invitations to dinner, and encouraging and heartfelt cards. She was willing to show how she felt that first week, while I tried to cover it up. Two years later she was a tenure-tracked teacher at that school, and I was interviewing for teaching jobs. It was a hard lesson, but one that I'll thankfully never forget.

Synonyms for help

If the word "help" is intimidating, there are synonyms listed below that may be easier to stomach. The main thing is not the word choice — it's that we ask!

Help
Advice
Collegiality
Collaboration
Educational Consulting
Professional Development

All these words describe the same thing: "show and tell." Working together is an essential element for teachers to survive and flourish. However skilled and inspired we feel inside, we could very well become stilted and burned out if we don't get in the habit of sharing with colleagues.

We receive the help we ask for

No matter what we name it, when we ask for help, magic happens. The first indication is that we receive the help we ask for. I have been asking for help from colleagues, administrators, and students for many years, many times a day, and I have never once been turned down.

One time, when I was a first-year teacher, I was about to be evaluated by the principal. It was my prep period and I was anxiously reviewing my lesson plan, when I realized trouble was ahead: I had planned my lesson around a book that I had forgotten to ask the students to bring to school! There was another teacher in the staff room at the time, but she was on the phone with her back to me. I meekly interrupted to ask if she could help me with my lesson plan, to which she replied, without turning around, "Sure. Why don't you check with me after school?"

"After school," I thought, "I'll have plenty of time, because I'll be out of a job." Aloud I said only, "Thank you." Something in my voice, some squeak or fluctuation of desperation, got through to her. She turned around, took one look at my face, and barked into the phone, "Gotta go. Teacher down! Hold my calls! Medic!!"

Needless to say, I received the help I needed just in the nick of time, and was able to keep my job. Otherwise this might be a manual on burger flipping strategies…

Openness is win-win

We've established the benefits to the teacher on the *receiving* end of assistance in a teaching environment, but there is also a flip-side in this exchange. Our openness can improve the experiences of the teachers on the *giving* end, who will appreciate not being cornered with a defensive colleague. If receiving help at first is challenging, think of the untenable position of a mentor offering help to a struggling, resistant, know-it-all, "Teflon teacher" — who allows suggestions to slide off un-received and untried.

And then remember the magic. Those who give us help blossom even more than we do. When they share their expertise, colleagues begin to reflect on their craft and appreciate what they know. Many principals and administrators seek to hire brand new teachers for this reason — to enliven a grade level or department with the collegial interaction that occurs when new teachers come on board. I believe that we learn most by teaching, whether it is teaching students or other teachers. Also, as professionals, we are all hungry to be acknowledged and appreciated. When asked for help, we receive that recognition and deepen our understanding and appreciation of our own skills as professionals.

Mrs. Allgood says

> Those who give us help blossom even more than we do.

Strategies

Help-ful tips for new teachers

There are several areas where new teachers don't yet "know the ropes." Having a heads up beforehand can make things a lot easier.

Share evaluations with trusted teachers

After receiving your evaluations from the administration, please share them with a mentor teacher/support provider, regardless of what the evaluations say. If there are one or more "needs improvements," then your mentor can help you hone in on the solutions. If the evaluation is excellent, you and your mentor can share a well-deserved sense of pride. Either way, the discussions centering on evaluations are often rich and insightful.

Read between the lines of evaluations

Like mentor teachers, administrators know that teachers like Mrs. Meanswell need encouragement. If a first evaluation were totally negative, Mrs. Meanswell might shut down and go into a shell, thereby limiting her opportunity for growth. So administrators often use the first evaluation more as a carrot than as a stick.

They emphasize the positive, with only a small percentage focusing on the negative, *even if the negative is enough to warrant end-of-the-year dismissal*. The potential problem is that Mrs. Meanswell needs to know clearly what is not satisfactory. Many times I've had to walk new teachers through their first evaluations, pointing out areas for improvement that the teachers thought to skip over, because the overall tone of the evaluation was so positive.

A Closer Look

Administrators often use the first evaluation more as a carrot than as a stick.

Document everything

Being open doesn't mean being naive. In addition to asking for help and sharing successes and challenges, being open also means being aware of potentially sticky situations, and dealing with them proactively. One strategy is to document all potentially controversial decisions, conversations, and actions. A simple way is to have a documentation notebook in which to record conversations and interactions with parents, administrators, students, and others. Simply note the date and time, a basic summary of the content of the interaction, and any direct quotes that might help down the line if someone might remember a conversation differently. Another way is to use an index card for each student. This makes it easier when gathering notes for parent conferences.

Transferring students to another class

Despite all our good intentions, our self-improvement, and suggestions from colleagues, sometimes outside intervention by the administration is appropriate, especially when students truly are in the wrong room. Unless we ask to reassign these students, we'll never know the potential positive impact for our classes.

I clearly remember one new sixth-grade teacher I was working with, who was having trouble with her third-period class. She told me that the class was out of control and that she would prefer that I observe her during a different period. After about two months, the teacher revealed a key source to the tumult of the third-period classroom: Samantha. Samantha wouldn't stay in her seat, would disrupt, not do homework, and would incite the other students. A month later, after much diplomacy on my part, the teacher allowed me to observe the class.

After ten minutes, it was obvious to me that Samantha was in the wrong place. She was clearly a special-needs student who had fallen through the cracks and was placed incorrectly. A week later, Samantha had gone to a more appropriate and nurturing environment, and the new teacher had a new lease on life. The sad news for everyone is that this didn't happen until early December.

Wise Apple Advice

Sometimes outside intervention by the administration is appropriate, especially when students truly are in the wrong room.

This example is not atypical. It happens fairly often in large school settings, and unfortunately the solution isn't always as straightforward as we would like. Sometimes the administration chooses not to move inappropriately placed students. But even then, by recognizing the truth of the situation and asking for help, at least the teacher knows what she's dealing with. In this unusually severe circumstance, she can adjust her expectations and her techniques to minimize conflict—for the other students and for herself.

Give students chances to ask for help

Teachers are not the only ones who need help in the classroom, but it is their job to pave the way for students to feel safe in asking for help. In Chapter 7, "Creating Positive Connections with Students," there are several suggestions for encouraging openness in students. Among them: suggestion boxes, community circles, and designated signals such as objects placed on desks or hand signals for students to utilize if they need us.

However we go about it, our mentorship in this area is crucial to addressing the needs of the student as a whole person. Our modeling openness certainly starts the process, but there is more we can do.

Remembering we are role models

We know that being open takes the edge off the challenges of being human. But being a teacher means being open to more than asking for help; it also means being a role model. Our students learn about themselves by measuring their experiences against those of people in their community. One of our jobs is simply being available to be seen as an adult out in the world.

Our openness to taking on this task is a quality that rubs off in our teaching and in our personal relationships with our students. This is equally true regardless of how old our students are. I remember one of my high school students once spotted me in the grocery store:

Student:	MR. SMITH!! WHAT ARE YOU DOING HERE?!??!!
Me:	Shopping.
Student:	SHOPPING!! OH MY GOODNESS, MY TEACHER IS SHOPPING!!
Me:	Well, the school lets me out on Saturdays for good behavior…

In that silly moment, I realized that the student had never thought of me outside the classroom. I had to let it be okay that he could look in my basket and see that I had a secret passion for "Count Chocula." This open approach helped immensely when the stakes were higher, when problems arose and feelings got hurt and solutions were necessary. My students began to trust the person I was, and to know they were safe with me.

5

GOT STRESS?

> *"Life is what happens to you while you're busy making other plans."*
>
> — JOHN LENNON

HERMANSEN

HOWEVER GOOD WE ARE AS TEACHERS, however prepared, positive, effective, and resilient, we are going to spend some up-close and personal time with the experience of stress. How we address this can make a big difference in our overall outlooks, attitudes, and successes as teachers — and as people. There certainly seems to be a correlation between how effective we are at reducing stress and how effective we are at managing our classes, regardless of our level of experience. Taking the time to address the causes of our stress and some possible antidotes isn't a luxury; it's a necessity. Veteran teachers please note: though this chapter is primarily oriented toward the stress of the new teacher, it's applicable across the board. The stress of the new teacher, if gone unchecked, manifests in the burnout of the veteran. Let's choose enthusiasm!

The Biggest Source of Teacher Stress

In my workshops I often ask participants what they think is the biggest source of stress for teachers. I get the full gamut of responses, ranging from writing lesson plans and grading papers, to talking with irate parents or dealing with kids who act out all the time. I suggest that none of these is the prime culprit. Nor is writing Individual Education Plans (IEPs), dealing with unforgiving administrators, or trying to get the class quiet. I suggest that the single biggest source of stress for teachers is

Unrealistic expectations of themselves.

Each of the individual stressors mentioned above is certainly part of teaching. But each of them can be stressful or not, depending on how we judge ourselves as teachers.

Granted, we need to work a lot of hours a day in order to teach well. But those hours can be a whole lot more relaxed if we aren't constantly looking over our shoulders, wondering if we're good enough, doing it right, pleasing the administration, or getting the kids to like us. And of course it's tough for new teachers because they don't really know what to expect. Here's a potent analogy:

Being a new teacher is like trying to fly an airplane… while building it.

New teachers have to take care of the daily "doingness" of teaching, such as planning lessons and grading papers. But they also have to figure out the big picture at the same time. Ever tried to put together one of those do-it-yourself bookshelves or rocking horses? Frustrating nightmare! Ever built a second one right after the first? Piece of cake! This is because we had to go through the process of learning the directions as we put the first one together. By the second time, the secret was out.

For the entire first year I taught, I was wrangling a dismantled Boeing 747. I was generally one day ahead of my students. I didn't mention to them that I had learned their day's lesson the night before; I naturally tried to impress upon them only how vital the information was, and how they couldn't live without it. I kept this desperate approach as an embarrassing secret until I later learned that I was right on track for a new teacher. My 747 was wobbly, with only two engines firing, but it was in the air.

With experience, teaching becomes easier. But how much experience does it take until we know the air-traffic controllers by name? When I was getting my credential, I was told some valuable information:

- ▲ The average teacher teaches the same thing three years in a row before "feeling comfortable" with it.
- ▲ The average teacher doesn't plateau in ability for seven years.

I would suggest that excellent teachers don't plateau at seven years. They *never* plateau. Such is the blessing and the curse of teaching—we can always do it better.

Our Infinite Job Description

The job description of a teacher is infinite. We can always put more red ink on our students' papers. We can always devote more time to our bulletin boards. We can always make more phone calls to parents. Our job is never-ending.

This is the *good news*. Why? For several reasons. First, if we find ourselves going to bed at night with a sense of incompleteness about our work, then we know we're right on track. Teachers who thrive in the profession know this feeling well, and have learned to accept and embrace it. Second, because we can't do everything, we shouldn't try. We will never dot every 'i' and cross every 't'. The nature of our job demands that we make choices, that in some areas we work as impeccably as we can, and in other areas we cut corners. Mrs. Allgood rarely complains about the fact that her job is never done. She recognizes the feeling of incompleteness as part of what it means to be a successful teacher. She picks per priorities, focuses on them, and lets the rest go. Third, crucial to her emotional health, she also knows that however good she is at classroom management, sometimes nothing she tries seems to work. This is simply part of what it means to be a teacher.

A Closer Look

Our job description is infinite – and this is the good news.

This news is especially pertinent for new teachers, because they often come into the profession thinking that they have to do it all. Since by definition "all" is unachievable, a rethinking is necessary. Otherwise, the new teacher will feel that she is falling farther and farther behind some mythical signpost of competence. Unlike actual planes, that classroom 747 may never have all its parts, but it flies well anyway.

Find What Works

There are countless self-help books and gurus out there with all sorts of advice on releasing, managing, using, avoiding, and thriving on stress. Much of the advice offered is wonderful, including getting enough rest, eating right, exercising, and spending time with loved ones. I recommend that teachers identify the things that work, and schedule them throughout the week regularly. Even if one effective technique is spontaneity, then schedule it in: "Tuesday, 8 PM, be spontaneous for one point three hours…" Otherwise, teachers may end up like I was during large parts of my first few years as a teacher. At times, I made school work so much more important than my "life," that periodically I'd wake up in the morning over the edge, in what I call "machine mode." No longer was I a person who taught. I had become a machine-teacher who was never quite good enough, who was in constant need of repair.

Five minutes a day

During my last teaching job, the bell would ring to end third period, and the kids would go flying out the door to be the first ones in line at the cafeteria. I would follow them, get my bagel and cream cheese, walk to the staff room, eat my bagel and cream cheese, and return to class just before the bell rang for fourth period. At some point in this cycle, it dawned on me that during break, *I was never resting.* I was being a robot, doing the "robot-break thing." So I decided to try something different, which worked so well I did it in one form or another every day.

When the bell would ring to signal break, after the kids had flown out of the room, I would do nothing. I would simply stand still, and begin to notice my feet — I tend to forget that I have feet when I'm teaching. I might stand still, I might walk slowly around the room, I might take my shoes off. Slowly I'd begin to notice my breath. What part of my body was receiving breath? I might walk slowly over to the window and look out at the trees to the right, not at the traffic to the left, and maybe gaze at the birds' nests that had been built in the corner of my windows. I would not return phone calls, make lists, grade papers, check on lesson plans — nothing to do directly with teaching. Invariably, after a few minutes, something shifted. I stopped being a machine that was behind, and returned to being a person who had chosen to teach. This five-minute shift was an invaluable vacation. I could then get my bagel and cream cheese and join the staff or join the students, but I would be so much more relaxed and resilient.

So my suggestion is:

Sometime during the day, take five minutes of unstructured time for yourself.

Disengage from the job description and remember yourself. Metaphorically step away from your role as teacher, and reconnect with yourself as a human being, rather than a human doing.

This is not as easy as it may seem. Finding five minutes during the school day is often quite difficult. It needs to be made a priority. Once at a school district function I shared this five-minute idea with a principal of a neighboring school. He decided to try it and reported great results. The only problem was that whenever I needed to contact him for school-related business, his reply was always, "Not now Rick, I'm doing my five minutes!"

Taking Care of Ourselves

On a Boeing 747, or even on a puddle-jumping prop, just before take-off the flight attendant once again instructs us about how to use a safety belt. Talk about teaching procedures! Then we are told that in the event of sudden cabin air pressure loss, an oxygen mask will drop from the ceiling. The kicker: that if we are traveling with a small child, we should put our mask on first, and then take care of the child. Why do we put our own mask on first? Because otherwise, both parent and child might lose consciousness.

Mrs. Allgood says

> We are human beings, not human doings.

The main reason we get so stressed as teachers is because we care so much about the success of our students. Therefore, it can be said that our caring gets us into stress. And, I would suggest, our caring can get us out. We have inside us a "laser beam" of caring that we often focus on our students. By refocusing our laser beam on ourselves, we can often greatly reduce our stress, without losing sight of our students' success and without losing our integrity. We need to slap that oxygen mask on our faces. Period. Even though we're in this for the kids. Even though education and schools are all about the kids. We can't give what we don't have. If we fail to monitor our own levels of stress, and we burn out in the name of going the extra mile, we are doing ourselves *and our students* a disservice. Ultimately, teachers who are good to themselves deliver the best teaching.

How do we take care of ourselves in the classroom? We can start by making the "unconscious" conscious, the "automatic" intentional. Several years ago while teaching in a credential program, I noticed that the Educational Psychology professor and I employed two distinctly different approaches. When a student teacher described a rough or problematic school situation, the psychologist always responded first with, "How did you feel?" When I was presented with the same scenario, my first question almost always was, "What did you do?"

Both questions are valid and essential, and they unravel our auto-pilot responses in stressful situations that are over before we've had a chance to think or reflect. I tend to side first with the question of action because as teachers we are responsible for our students. To me, this manifests as a constant need to do things, to take care of situations, regardless of how we feel. However, if we also don't actively address our feelings, we can end up reacting in ways we don't want to — thereby undermining the very relationships we're trying to cultivate.

My approach is to "check in" regularly with my feelings — the good, the bad, and the ugly — with a trusted colleague, mentor teacher, or friend. Others prefer a more solitary approach. Whatever way works best for us, the point is to balance our emotional responses with our actions so that we are responsive and resilient, and our students receive consistency.

And outside the classroom? Imagine it's a Tuesday evening at about eight o'clock, and you're at home with a stack of papers to grade. The phone rings and it's your friend asking you to drop everything and "go out." The angel on your right shoulder says, "Stay home and be responsible. Grade the papers." The devil on your left shoulder shouts, "GO OUT!" "Grade papers," says the angel. "Go out," implores the devil. What should you do?

My answer? At least every once in a while, go out. Not only will you be benefiting yourself, but you may be benefiting your students as well. Research suggests that:

> *Wise Apple Advice*
>
> Our caring gets us into stress – our caring can get us out.

"The more positive students' perceptions are of their teacher's feelings, the better the academic achievement and the more desirable their classroom behavior, as rated by the teacher. (Clarke and Brookover)"

In regular English, this means that if students sense that their teacher feels good, they will behave better and will perform better academically. So if going out every once in a while allows us to exhale in our lives, puts a smile on our face and brings us back into the classroom more relaxed and resilient, then please, by all means, let's go for it. Even though we won't have the students' papers corrected, our presence will be a much more positive factor in the classroom. We can always cite the above research and tell them that we were helping them succeed by not grading their papers...

The bottom line of expectations

A Closer Look

If students sense that their teacher feels good, they will behave better and will perform better academically.

With all of this focus on teacher relaxation, self-esteem, taking time to remember we have feet, what's the bottom line? What are realistic expectations that a new teacher ought to have for her first year?

If, after your first year of teaching, you want to continue in the profession, and if, after your first year of teaching, the administration wants you to return, then you have had a successful first year.

Granted, there is a lot of room for new teacher performance above and beyond this bottom line. But this is the "bones." Sometimes in working with new teachers, I see them get so concerned about the minutiae that they forget to take a look every once in a while at the big picture. Yes it's important to give each student the proper grade, and yes it's important to fill out all of the various forms correctly and make sure that Maria doesn't sit next to Johnny and Mark stays after school 4.3 minutes. But in the end, the bottom line is: Do you want to come back? Do they want you to come back? You'll improve dramatically in your second year. You'll improve dramatically in your third year. As long as you leave open the possibility of returning so that you can improve, you're on the right track.

Mrs. Allgood says

Welcome all the feelings of incompletion and inadequacy that inevitably come from this profession, but don't listen to them too closely.

Ask Mrs. Allgood how her first teaching years were. She will most likely laugh to herself or sigh, and admit how difficult they were. In the next breath, she'll affirm how glad she is that she stayed with it.

Stress before the December holidays

Even though the kids seem excited about the holidays, they are often more stressed than usual. Their vacation expectations are too high, or they may have tough family situations and fear losing the stability of school during the break. But they are not alone; many teachers ruefully admit that they don't get sick except during vacations. This seems especially true for the December holidays. In each of my first three years, I taught right up until the Friday before vacation, fighting a cold or sore throat, only to lose the fight on the first day of vacation.

After years of struggle, I came up with a solution. I made a conscious decision not to eat any sweets between Thanksgiving and the December break, because the influx of holiday sugar seemed to lower my immune system. I kept my hands off parents' cakes, the PTA's pies, and the kids' candy canes and chocolate. I seemed to cope better with all the stresses of the vacation and the new winter germs — and I stopped getting sick.

Wise Apple Advice

A final word on stress

Take care of yourself and you can take care of your students. Remember to be as soft with yourself as you are with your students in your very best moments. Welcome all the feelings of incompletion and inadequacy that inevitably come from this profession, but don't listen to them too closely. We are role models. Modeling this awareness, resiliency, and openness while truly enjoying ourselves is one of the greatest gifts we can give our students.

PREVENTION – What We Do Proactively

"*An ounce of prevention is worth a pound of detention.*"

6

HOLDING
OUR GROUND

> *"What gives light
> must endure burning."*
> —VIKTOR FRANKL

WHEN MRS. ALLGOOD tells a student to do something, he does it. When she gives a student a consequence for inappropriate behavior, the student does not erupt with unnecessary protests or complaining. Although we might not be able to see some obvious reason why that student responds so well to Mrs. Allgood's directions, there is something going on underneath the surface that is making all the difference. I call this Mrs. Allgood's ability to hold her ground.

Holding our ground is challenging, regardless of the system of rules and consequences we have, regardless of the grade we teach, and regardless of the ability or attitude of our students. This invisible quality, this willingness to be firm without being mean, spills into everything we do as teachers. It influences the way we enforce consequences, the way we impart information, describe procedures, talk with students about their lives, walk down the hall, even how we feel about ourselves and our jobs. Imagine a typical classroom situation where the students want one thing

Mrs. Allgood says

> Our willingness to be firm without being mean spills into everything we do as teachers.

and we want another. If we can hold our ground with our students without beating them up, without beating ourselves up, without having to go home that night and recover, and in a way that invites student cooperation, then we have succeeded at the hardest element of classroom management.

How does one learn to hold one's ground effectively? While various components are sprinkled throughout this book, perhaps the most primary is our ability to say "No" — what we do — while remaining on our students' side — who we are.

The Firm and Soft Paradox

When Mrs. Allgood disciplines a student, three things are evident:

- ▲ Her voice goes down in volume
- ▲ Her voice goes lower in tone
- ▲ Her body more squarely faces the student

These characteristics offer the student a chance to save face while shifting his behavior. There is a constant de-escalation in the way she holds her ground.

For example, if Mrs. Allgood is teaching a math lesson and Mark is playing with a magazine, she stops, internally assumes the best about Mark — that he wants to learn behavior (Chapter 2, "Assume the Best"). She then faces Mark squarely, and quietly in a low tone asks him to please put the magazine away. He feels invited, rather than challenged. With her posture, volume, and tone, Mrs. Allgood communicates that she is firm in her resolve, yet soft — she is on Mark's side. Once Mark knows this, in later occurrences she often doesn't need to say anything. Just facing him can be enough. Further, whenever possible, Mrs. Allgood addresses Mark privately. This is addressed more thoroughly later in Chapter 12, "Rules and Consequences."

Saying "No"

In my classroom management workshops, I create an artificial situation where participants pair off and role-play. One person becomes a teacher, and another becomes a student in that teacher's class. The student's job is to get the teacher to allow him to leave the classroom, using whatever compelling reasons he can think of. The teacher's job is to communicate that the student can't leave. No matter what. Even if the reasons are about life and death. I implement this role-play to make conscious the emotional charge that teachers feel in moments of conflict with students. These moments are where we can best examine our strengths and challenges.

At one point in the role-play, I limit the teacher's vocabulary to two possible word-for-word responses:

No.

I understand, and the answer is No.

Afterwards, we talk about the teachers' experiences and identify several successful approaches.

Don't Over-explain

First, most of the time, teachers don't need to explain why they are holding their ground with their students. In situations where they do need to explain, most likely they don't need to explain right away.

When we explain our reasons right away, invariably the student will provide a reason that he feels is better, even if his reasoning is bizarre. This is simply biology. Students seem to have "argue!" built into their genetic code (teams of DNA researchers have discovered this vital fact about humans between the ages of two and eighteen). No matter what students ask, they have an investment in receiving a "yes" answer, and they can't help but react when we hold our ground. When we say, "No, Mark, you can't go to your locker right now," Mark will blurt out a meaningless singsong syllable that sounds something like:

Wha... Wha... WHY!!

This "why" is most often an emotive blurt rather than a logical query. If we try to answer the question logically, the student will slip out of "right-brain-emotive-blurt" mode and jump into "left-brain-logical-debate-and-argue" mode. Before long, this debate becomes the class lesson. Twenty or thirty pairs of eyes are watching it unfold. Pretty soon, kids will be calling out from the back of the room, "Let him go! He's right! Let him go!" Or just as bad, "Let's vote!" If this sounds familiar, then welcome to the teacher's nightmare: the "land of reasons."

The solution? Table any explanation until later. Get the conflict off center stage. Ask the student to approach you "in ten minutes when the bell rings" or "in four minutes after we start the art work" or "in six minutes when we line up for recess." Getting the discussion out of the "moment" will keep more students on task, eliminate the involvement of "student lawyers," and de-escalate issues to a time when cooler heads will prevail.

Giving the student options, such as, "talk to me after school or at lunch tomorrow," puts the onus on the student to come to us. Otherwise we might forget and the student could perceive that as a slight. If and when you do explain, speak one-on-one to your student, out of earshot of others. When explanations are tabled, however, most of the time students won't end up asking why. The reason is not that they are intimidated or cynical, but because once they have a couple of minutes to allow the dust to settle, they realize why — or they realize they don't particularly care why — and they settle down to work.

Alternatives to tabling explanations are repeating the initial answer, or simply waiting silently. The silent option can be accompanied by gestures, such as pointing to or looking at what-ever the student should be doing.

The word "No" isn't what's critical; it's what it symbolizes. In fact, we never need to use "No" in order to hold our ground without explaining: "Yes, Mark, you can use the bathroom, as soon as the bell rings."

Avoiding an explanation does not correlate to a lack of caring for students. To underscore this fact, add simple sentences that go a long way: "I hear that you are very concerned, Maria. I see that this matters to you. I'll tell you what: please do have a seat now, and then come talk to me as soon as everyone starts working on their projects. Let's see then what we can work out." Caring does not equal explaining; our commitment to fairness and compassion does not mean we have to have open debates with our students about decisions we've made.

Mrs. Allgood says

Table explanations until later – get conflicts off center stage.

Characteristics of an Effective "No"

Mrs. Allgood's "No" is effective, yet at first glance, we can't see why. However, when we carefully compare her technique to Mrs. Meanswell's, we can start to discern vital differences.

An effective "No" has **no blame**. Mrs. Allgood doesn't blame Mark for the fact that he wants to page through a magazine, or leave the classroom, or talk with his neighbor. She simply communicates to him what needs to happen instead.

An effective "No" has **no complaining**. She doesn't complain, either under her breath or out loud, when Mark talks out of turn. She simply communicates to him that it is not appropriate.

An effective "No" has **no wiggle room**. When she holds her ground, she doesn't leave open any loopholes for Mark to try to squeeze through. She simply and clearly communicates that the answer is no.

An effective "No" has **no animosity, baiting, antagonism, waf-fling, sarcasm, attack, equivocation, or humiliation.** It is simple, clear, to the point, and expedient.

Ambiguous Characteristics of "No"

There are some surprising, even counter-intuitive characteristics of an effective "No."

An effective "No" might have **hesitation.** Sometimes a student asks us something, and we honestly don't know what to decide.

A Closer Look

Caring does not equal explaining

No problem. We can simply ask the student to ask again at a later time: "I'm not sure, José. Please ask me again at the end of group work and I'll let you know then." If we assume that we should never be unsure of an answer, then we might pick an answer right away that we'll end up having to defend later. There's nothing wrong with changing our minds either. Holding our ground is not about being rigid. It's more about our presence and inner authority as we respond flexibly to various situations.

An effective "No" might require an immediate **explanation.** There is no "one-size-fits-all" rule about this. It's just that Mrs. Meanswell tends to over-explain, thus getting her into trouble unnecessarily.

An effective "No" might very well involve feelings, such as **anger** or **guilt.** Just about all teachers have felt these emotions in the classroom. We might have a student that just ticks us off, or there might be a school policy that we don't agree with but have to enforce anyway. If we push these feelings away, they can come back to haunt us.

Anger vs. Reactivity

Let's say Mark is tapping his pencil, giggling, and calling out, and has triggered a feeling of anger inside us. If we think, "Good teachers are never supposed to feel angry," we'll try to overcome our anger by squelching or avoiding it. As we spend our energy this way and Mark continues to bother us, we will inevitably start to see him as the enemy. He is the one who is forcing us to feel inappropriate feelings. Soon blame will follow, along with either our snapping at him or being sarcastic. It goes something like this:

Externally:	"Mark, please stop talking and have a seat.
Internally:	(I won't be angry I won't be angry I won't be angry. Anger isn't okay. Anger is for bad teachers.)
Externally:	"Mark, I said please stop talking and have a seat."
Internally:	(Stop making me angry! Anger is wrong! Stop doing this to me!)
Externally:	"MARK!!!"

A Closer Look

Anger is a *feeling* – reactivity is a choice.

This type of response is what I call reactivity. It is different from anger in that anger is a feeling that we all have from time to time. Like the weather, it comes and goes. Reactivity, on the other hand, is a choice that we make to take our anger out on someone — often ourselves.

What's the alternative? We simply take a deep breath and count to ten before responding. In that time of counting to ten, we re-assume the best about Mark and ourselves: that he wants to learn behavior, and that part of our job is to teach him appropriate behavior (this is explained more fully in Chapter 2, "Assume the Best"). We should remember that he is not out to get us, but instead he is simply communicating that he hasn't fully learned how to behave appropriately.

After counting to ten, look inside, welcome the anger, and simply state in a calm voice what Mark needs to do. Don't squelch the anger. Simply note it, avoid blaming anyone for it, and then act calmly and professionally.

Counting to ten, in and of itself, is often not enough. Many teachers tell me that the longer they count, the angrier they get! Remembering while we count that our students want to learn behavior is the key.

When I first started teaching, counting to ten wasn't enough. I often had to count a lot higher. Sometimes at night I'd get a phone call from a friend asking to go out, but I'd respond, "I can't. I'm too busy counting." Now, I don't necessarily get angry with students *less frequently*, it's just no longer as big a deal. When I am angry, I find I usually don't have to count to ten. I just need to take one deep breath, during which I make the choice to assume the best about my student, and then I express what I need to — without blowing up, without blaming the student for making me angry, and without blaming myself for being angry.

We can allow ourselves these natural feelings of anger, guilt, or anxiety, and yet not indulge or act them out. When these feelings knock on our door,

Let's let them in for tea— but not serve them a seven-course meal!

What about situations where we can't calm down in time, and yet we have to discipline a student? If it's not a question of physical safety, I'd suggest leaning in the direction of keeping our mouths shut until it's possible we can speak non-reactively with the student. If we react, regardless of our good intentions, we will communicate to the student that

- ▲ We are frustrated at our own feelings of helplessness
- ▲ The classroom is not safe
- ▲ The student is not welcome

We will win the battle. That is, the offending student will most likely do our bidding. But we will then find ourselves in a land of battles. We will come to school on the defensive and preparing for confrontation instead of magic.

What happens if we get in a pattern of reactivity with our students? Hopefully, we'll be able to break the pattern by being responsive rather than reactive. But if we continually react with students, several things may well happen:

- ▲ We will start to assume the worst about our students, rather than the best.
- ▲ They will become "bad kids" to us, rather than good kids making unwise choices.
- ▲ We will start looking for and seeing evidence to support this.
- ▲ Our students will start to reflect this negative assumption, by acting out more and challenging more, or by ceasing participation in class discussions and activities.
- ▲ Ultimately, if our students feel powerless and intimidated enough, it's possible that as a call for help, they will start spreading rumors, including accusing us of things we haven't actually done.

A Closer Look

If we react, we will win the battle. But we'll find ourselves in a land of battles.

These symptoms aren't the end of the world. But they are "yellow lights" in our universe. They are warning signals to take full responsibility for our feelings, to re-choose positive assumptions about ourselves and our students, and to regain their trust step-by-step through calm, clear, firm, and non-reactive communication and use of consequences.

In this circumstance, we also may need to explore our use of apology. Recognizing when and how to incorporate the dynamic of apology is a fine art. Please refer to Chapter 3, "Inner Authority," for an expanded discussion of apology.

7

POSITIVE
CONNECTIONS

*"Teaching is not just hard work,
it's 'heart' work."*

—ELEISE BUXTON

IN ORDER FOR Mrs. Allgood to work her magic in the classroom, to create an environment where students trust and
learn from her, she cultivates positive, healthy connections
with her students. This goal is both a frame of mind and a series
of decisions that together, with practice, meld into intuition —
and then into action. Let's break positive connections down into
visible, workable pieces.

The Ingredients – Caring

If we personally and genuinely care for our students, they'll
know and appreciate us, no matter what classroom management
menus we use, no matter what our teaching style.

A major concern of mine as a new teacher was my ability to
communicate to my students that I genuinely cared for them. I
spent many long conversations in credential courses discussing
the best strategies for succeeding at this. Then once I had my own
class, it began to slowly dawn on me what I already knew: name-
ly, that caring isn't a strategy, it's a choice. I began to realize that

my students knew I cared for them, even when my lessons bombed and when they walked all over me. The hard part of this realization: the fact that they knew I cared for them didn't stop them from acting out and taking advantage of my management loopholes.

Some of the Mrs. Allgoods out there are tough. We wonder how they can be quite firm and yet their students still feel cared for. It's because their genuine caring underlies all that they do.

Doing what's best, not what's easiest

It is our job to assume that regardless of what they claim, our students want what serves them best — what they most *need*. This doesn't mean that we shouldn't truly consider student opinion. It just means that we shouldn't be giving kids ice cream and cake for every meal.

A Closer Look

If we genuinely care for our students, they'll know it, regardless of how they behave.

Teachers often confuse being nice with being kind. This can get them into trouble. In my vernacular, being nice means doing things to get the kids to like us. Being kind means doing things that are truly in the students' best interest. Sometimes they translate into doing the same thing. For example, if students are obviously struggling with a new lesson, and Mrs. Meanswell gives the kids a break in order to avoid her own feelings of insecurity, then she is choosing to be nice. If, on the other hand, Mrs. Allgood gives the kids a break in order to give them an opportunity to approach the lesson from a new and fresh perspective later, she is making a decision more in line with being kind.

Even though their decisions are the same, the difference in motivation is critical. The kids in Mrs. Meanswell's class are in charge, using a silent threat of dissatisfaction as a way to manipulate her. Ultimately they will exercise their power — their reactions to her choices — in ways that are off-task, and thus confrontational. And, because the students actually do want to learn, they will eventually start acting out because they won't be satisfied. They will complain about all sorts of things, as a veiled communication that what they really want are structure, direction, and learning. They want Mrs. Meanswell to steer in a way that's in their best interest.

And when steering includes discipline, Mrs. Allgood's direct, matter-of-fact style reflects her understanding of this truth. Her words leave very little wiggle room, and while students might make a show of wiggling, they respond to her. This is because she focuses on what's best for them, and knows that the students need it.

The underlying message is that teachers need to be firmly committed to what the students need, even if that means occasionally experiencing feelings of being disliked or under-appreciated. The students will be better served, and they will actually appreciate the teacher more, even if they don't express it.

> *A Closer Look*
>
> When we act to get the kids to like us, we give them our power. When we choose to be kind, we exercise our power.

Head, heart, and gut

This is still another "road map" for looking at what the teacher experiences vs. what the teacher chooses to do (not all teachers find this map valuable, so don't worry if it doesn't feel like a good fit).

The head is what we **think**. The heart is what we **feel**. The gut is what we **know**. Often, students speak from their head or their heart, wanting something that isn't always what they know they need. As teachers, we do the same, jumping back and forth between all three modalities. What I sometimes do in situations of confusion is to "check-in" with my gut, to see what I know needs to happen. It can help me cut through all the noise about wanting to be liked or wanted. I can also "check-in" with the bellies of individual students. Occasionally, I can be direct with students and ask them what they think, what they feel, and what they know about a given situation. It's surprising how often I will get honest answers from students when I frame things this way.

As I improved as a classroom manager, I found myself speaking more directly to what my students knew, rather than getting into a debate about what students thought they wanted, or who did what. For example:

Mark:	Mr. Smith, I don't think you're being fair. Lots of other kids were talking. Why did you pick on me?
Mr. Smith:	Mark, you and I both know that you want to improve your behavior. Right?
Mark:	Well, I guess so…
Mr. Smith:	That's why I'm here talking to you, so that we can work together to improve it.

Because I'm speaking directly to what Mark knows (his gut), he has to struggle in order to disagree with me. Oftentimes his complaints are short-circuited before he even knows what happened. If I come **at** him, then I run straight into his wave of defenses. But if I assume the best about him and speak to what he knows, I can come in **under** his wave, providing clarity and support simultaneously.

> Because I'm speaking directly to what Mark knows (his gut), he has to struggle in order to disagree with me.

Using these tools — from the analytical to the emotional to the instinctual — we can make good, solid choices when interacting with our students. And from this foundation, we can implement strategies to create strong positive connections with them.

When students feel a positive connection with the teacher and the class, they are more likely to participate and less likely to act out. Ongoing personal connections between teachers and students serve as continual invitations for students to step out of resistance and into cooperation and learning.

The Recipe – Strategies

Choices

The more we can build in choices for our students, the more likely they are to feel energized as participants in their learning process. Mrs. Meanswell can start by asking herself the following question every time she finishes designing a lesson:

Where can I build in choices for my students in this lesson?

Often, the answer to this question is "nowhere."

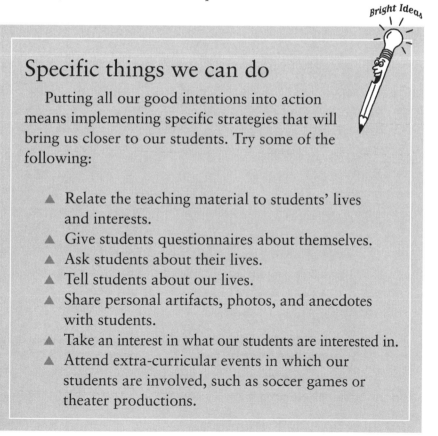

Specific things we can do

Putting all our good intentions into action means implementing specific strategies that will bring us closer to our students. Try some of the following:

- ▲ Relate the teaching material to students' lives and interests.
- ▲ Give students questionnaires about themselves.
- ▲ Ask students about their lives.
- ▲ Tell students about our lives.
- ▲ Share personal artifacts, photos, and anecdotes with students.
- ▲ Take an interest in what our students are interested in.
- ▲ Attend extra-curricular events in which our students are involved, such as soccer games or theater productions.

But by asking consistently, we can often find ways. For example, Mrs. Meanswell can say to her class "We're going to do three things in this lesson. Which would you like to do first?" Students can vote, or a "Student of the Day" can decide. Mrs. Meanswell can give a quiz with twelve questions, and ask the students to pick their favorite ten questions to answer. Assigning homework is another example. Instead of assigning problems 1-10, she can let the students vote on doing either the evens or the odds for problems 1-20. Or, she can let each student pick any 8 problems of the 20 to do for homework. Even these simple options give students an added sense of participation and connection.

Small steps at first will lead to bigger steps, such as choices in assignments and activities, students teaching one another,

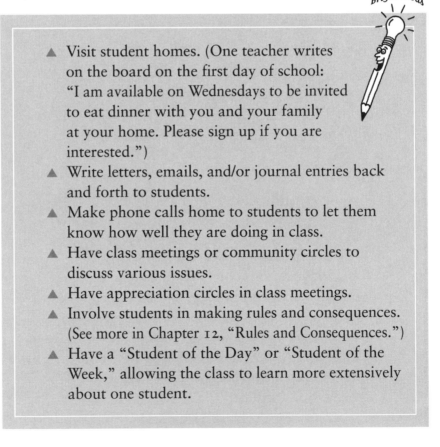

Bright Ideas

- ▲ Visit student homes. (One teacher writes on the board on the first day of school: "I am available on Wednesdays to be invited to eat dinner with you and your family at your home. Please sign up if you are interested.")
- ▲ Write letters, emails, and/or journal entries back and forth to students.
- ▲ Make phone calls home to students to let them know how well they are doing in class.
- ▲ Have class meetings or community circles to discuss various issues.
- ▲ Have appreciation circles in class meetings.
- ▲ Involve students in making rules and consequences. (See more in Chapter 12, "Rules and Consequences.")
- ▲ Have a "Student of the Day" or "Student of the Week," allowing the class to learn more extensively about one student.

and community service projects. Over time, as we include an aware-ness of student choice in our lesson design, we will find many ways to build it in.

The "4-H strategy" combines choices with personal connec-tions. When the teacher greets the students at the door, they choose one of four greetings: **h**ello, **h**andshake, **h**igh-five, or **h**ug (guess which option secondary teachers often forego). Students change their choices depending on their mood. Regardless of what they choose, they get a personal greeting from the teacher each day.

Make sure that you can live with whatever options students choose. This is addressed in more detail in Chapter 12: "Rules and Consequences."

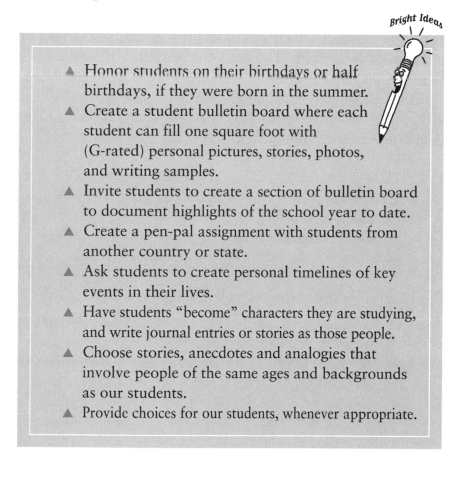

Bright Ideas

▲ Honor students on their birthdays or half birthdays, if they were born in the summer.
▲ Create a student bulletin board where each student can fill one square foot with (G-rated) personal pictures, stories, photos, and writing samples.
▲ Invite students to create a section of bulletin board to document highlights of the school year to date.
▲ Create a pen-pal assignment with students from another country or state.
▲ Ask students to create personal timelines of key events in their lives.
▲ Have students "become" characters they are studying, and write journal entries or stories as those people.
▲ Choose stories, anecdotes and analogies that involve people of the same ages and backgrounds as our students.
▲ Provide choices for our students, whenever appropriate.

Secondary teachers' built-in challenge

Secondary teachers generally have a tougher job at making connections with individual kids, because they have so many students each day. If a teacher of one hundred and fifty students spent all day speaking privately with one student after the next — without spending any time teaching lessons — she would have just over a minute and a half to spend with each student. Because we have to teach, that time is reduced to just a few seconds per day per student. Sad as it is, this is often all the time we have to make and reinforce a personal connection with each student (I sometimes joke that as a high school teacher, I became a master at the meaningful twenty-second conversation, which helped to support my cocktail party skills). In spite of this built-in limitation, meaningful and valuable personal contact can and does happen between teacher and student in ten and twenty-second connections. It's not always apparent based on the content of the conversations — for nonverbal communication is equally if not more significant. As we assume the best about ourselves and our students, these brief connections can communicate our caring in significant ways.

Bright Ideas

▲ Solicit student opinions on classroom, school, or global issues.
▲ Learn about our students' cultures and family histories.
▲ Honor our students' cultures and languages.
▲ Create community service opportunities for students.
▲ Set up cross-age tutoring for students.
▲ Provide regular opportunities for listening to students.
▲ Express genuine appreciation for students whenever appropriate.

Writing vs. speaking

When I taught at-risk high school students, I often would give them evaluation forms to fill out regarding units or projects that we had just completed. One day I included an optional question: "Is there anything that you would like me to know about you, this class, or anything else?" More than half my students left this question blank. But I did receive answers like, "Mr. Smith, I had a huge fight last night with my mom" or "Mr. Smith, I haven't slept at home in three days," and even "Mr. Smith, I really like this class."

I had previously met with these same students one-on-one and asked them how they were doing and what had been happening in their lives. In our personal conversations, all I heard was, "Fine. I'm doing fine." Somehow, students felt more comfortable confiding in me through the written word. Needless to say, I spent time with each student who had confided to me in writing, and a lot of good came from those conversations.

From then on, I always included that optional question at the end of all my unit evaluations. And each time, I received answers that surprised, enlightened, or tickled me.

Avoiding Pitfalls

As teachers, we wear many hats. By choosing to actively take part in all our many roles without complaint and with a positive attitude, we avoid a lot of problems and increase our opportunities for enjoying our jobs and serving our students.

Getting too personal

With rare exceptions, personal equals positive. The exception is when we cross a privacy line, by asking too much of our students or revealing too much about ourselves.

We all have a desire to connect personally with our students. Where, then, is that line between being friendly and being intrusive? There is no clear-cut answer. But paradoxically, the more willing we are to be firm and hold our ground with our students, the more personal we can be with them, without crossing that line. Our firmness allows the students to relax when we are soft, because they know that we are not abdicating our responsibilities to teach content and behavior. It is a balancing act, much like the seesaw below. The more weight put on one side, the more weight needs to be put on the other.

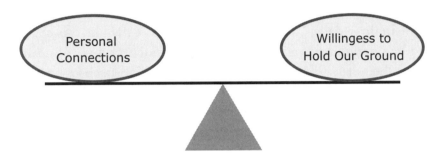

Let's look at how this works with Mrs. Meanswell. She is still new at developing her inner authority, so she is close to the center of the seesaw on the right side. She tries to compensate for this by being quite personal with her students. Sometimes this backfires. Perhaps she talks about things that are uncomfortable for the students, and

Mrs. Allgood says

> The more willing we are to be firm and hold our ground with our students, the more personal we can be with them, without crossing that line.

they express their discomfort through acting out at odd times. Or perhaps the kids feel overly friendly with her, and make it hard for her to quiet them down. She discovers, for example, that if she tells a joke, several minutes of chaos often follow, as kids go off-task to tell their own jokes. She has them in good spirits, but she doesn't seem to be able to establish sufficient focus. On the other hand, Mrs. Allgood's students seem quite comfortable with her "personalness." Even though she rarely "lays down the law" with her students, they know that *she is willing to do so*, and that she is committed to holding the line. Therefore they tend to act out less.

Prepare for the worst – assume the best

The art of teaching involves a kind of "realistic optimism" or "idealistic pragmatism" or "gullible integrity." I remember when I was Trick-or-Treating as a kid with my friends, and coming upon a house that had a bowl of Nestles Crunch bars outside the front door, with a note that read, "Parents: Happy Halloween. Sorry we couldn't be here personally to hand out candy. Please take one for each of your children." Did we take one each or empty the bowl? Suffice it to say that my bag had an overabundance of Nestles products that night — and for many nights afterwards. Did I know better? Yes. Did I feel guilty? Yes. Did I take the candy anyway? You betcha!

Mrs. Allgood says

Kids will be kids — we can give them room to spread their wings, as long as we're prepared with a safety net.

As teachers, we need to structure success for our students. Part of this means building in tailored options for our students, being realistic about how much independence our students can handle, and anticipating worst-case scenarios.

What could go wrong? Am I ready for it? If I word my questions/directions a certain way, what are possible misinterpretations that my students may make? Are my deadlines clear? What if some students finish early? What if they arrive late? What if the overhead projector doesn't work? The VCR? What if my substitute teacher isn't strong? What if kids fight in my room? What if there's a fire? Am I prepared for all these possibilities? Do I know what to do? Do I know what to say? How can I be ready in advance? Who can help me prepare?

Part of structuring success is addressed in the Before-School-Checklist in Chapter 10, "Getting Ready." Part of it is addressed in Chapter 8, "Teaching Procedures." And part of it is an attitude or orientation that we can bring to each situation.

We are the boss. Period.

One key to a successful, proactive attitude is gaining comfort with our position as teachers. We are in charge. In other words, there is a certain emotional or psychological charge that comes with being the boss, the keeper of the guidelines and the grades. And we are smack dab in the middle of that charge. Being the boss doesn't mean that we should be mean — just clear and firm in our resolve.

Mrs. Allgood says

> The sooner we embrace being the boss, the sooner we can succeed.

Authority is a double-edged sword. It's *great* because ultimately, as "authors" in our classrooms, we have more ability to craft our classroom environment than we might think. It's *difficult* because we are responsible for our classroom climate, no matter which students we teach. Even teachers who promote democratic and/or consensus-based classrooms are still "the boss." They are the ones with veto power. They are the ones who have held their ground so that their students respect them enough to feel safe in a democratically-run classroom.

The sooner we embrace this part of our job description, the sooner we can become successful teachers. But it isn't always easy. The fact that we are the boss can give rise to many feelings, both positive and negative — and *feelings drive actions*. How we address our feelings can make the difference between a bumpy and a smooth teaching experience. Let's look at some common scenarios.

There will be times when we are not liked — hated, even

This is inevitable, at least in our perception. Students may respond to us by blurting out, "You're mean," or "I hate you." It helps to know that this may happen from time to time, and that it doesn't necessarily mean that anything has gone wrong. Expressing feelings such as hatred or anger can be an essential part of a student's growth. If he feels received and not attacked for it, he often is so appreciative that his "negative" feelings transform rapidly into gratitude. Below is an all-too-common example.

| Teacher: | Mark, please put your pictures away and have a seat. |
| Mark: | You're mean! My other teachers are a lot nicer! |

At this moment, if a teacher were to resist Mark's opinion of her, it could lead to her being reactive, arguing with him in class, and generally creating the worst-case scenario that she is trying to avoid.

Mrs. Meanswell: MARK! I'M TIRED OF YOUR ATTITUDE! SIT DOWN!!!

In this example, Mrs. Meanswell ends up acting mean, just as Mark predicts. Her reactivity can be classified under many headings, such as "taking the bait," "having one's buttons pushed," "attacking," or "losing it." In defending herself from being seen a certain way, she is resisting certain possible judgments or opinions. "I can't be seen as mean. Therefore I need to cut out the source of those opinions quickly." Then Mark, who is perceived to be the source of those opinions, feels cut out.

Mrs. Allgood *responds* to Mark, instead of *reacting*.

| Mrs. Allgood: | Mark, please put your pictures away and have a seat. Otherwise you and I will need to meet after class. |

Here, Mrs. Allgood allows the consequences to speak for her—and Mark knows that meeting with her after class may entail further consequences. She doesn't react to Mark's reactivity, nor does she attack him back. After the dust settles, she can talk to him, letting him know that his antagonistic language is not acceptable.

Circumventing potentially reactive situations is discussed in Chapter 6, "Holding Our Ground." A few reminders: Count to ten. Take a deep breath. Re-orient with the positive assumption that the student wants to learn behavior. Do whatever it takes.

Know that if we can wait to talk with our student until we are calm, we've got a much better chance of genuinely communicating with him, thus decreasing tense classroom scenes in the future.

The emotional charge-transfer game

Question: Why is it that sometimes we leave school at the end of the day feeling beaten up, like we want to go home, close the blinds, and sit in the dark? Answer: Kids dump their emotional charge on us if we take the bait by reacting when they push our buttons. We go home exhausted, and they go home ready for more.

Let's look at the above example with Mark. Say he has had a huge fight with his parents that morning. He comes to school feeling angry, hurt, and bottled up with a strong emotional charge. When he lashes out at Mrs. Meanswell in class, he is signaling that he doesn't quite know how to address this charge in a healthy way. When she reacts, his experience "sticks" to her. It's as if she starts to feel his feelings. Mrs. Meanswell ends up feeling beaten up, as if she just went the wrong way over a driveway that reads, "Do not enter — severe tire damage." Mark feels justified in blaming her, and has a temporary reprieve whereby he feels permission to "dump" on others to get rid of his feelings. In this exchange, Mark loses out on the opportunity to address his emotional needs directly, and Mrs. Meanswell loses out on the opportunity to support him by modeling responsive behavior. And although his antagonism may be a cry for help, she misses the chance to perhaps talk to him about what is happening in his life.

A Closer Look

Kids dump their emotional charge on us if we react when they push our buttons. We go home exhausted, and they go home ready for more.

In my first three years of teaching, it seemed like I did Ph.D. work in reacting to students. I'd argue with and threaten them, yell out of frustration, or blame them for not participating. Only after years of teaching was I able to reorient, assume the best about them, and discover that many of my conflicts with students were actually opportunities to serve them.

Classes have no memory (though kids do)

Although some individual students will remember strong positive or negative classroom experiences — even if they don't let us know — the class as a whole is another animal. It has a short memory, which can be both a blessing and a curse.

We can have the most horrific experience with our students on Tuesday, and on Wednesday, they return as if the slate were totally clean. Similarly, no matter how wonderful our lesson is, when the bell rings, they are ready to go. We can count on a built-in resiliency in our classes, and therefore we are generally best served not "riding" on the good experiences or making too much over the bad ones. Our best recourse for success with our classes is cultivating strong positive connections.

8

TEACHING PROCEDURES

> *"A teacher is one who makes herself progressively unnecessary."*
>
> — THOMAS CARRUTHERS

Mrs. Meanswell knows that the bottom line for her success is how well her students learn content. So that's where she puts her focus. She doesn't realize the invaluable secret Mrs. Allgood has worked seamlessly into her system. Procedures, far from "busy work" or a distraction from content, are her best friends. Spending time on procedures in the classroom not only makes the environment run more smoothly, but it actually *facilitates* teaching content. Mrs. Allgood puts a tremendous emphasis on procedures, regardless of what grade level she teaches. Her procedures, ranging from how students enter the classroom, to how paper is distributed, to how pencils are sharpened, are taught, reinforced, practiced, and reviewed throughout the school year.

Here's a challenge I like to give teachers: I dare them to try to over-teach procedures. I imagine it's possible to do, but in the well over one hundred teachers I have observed and coached, I have never seen it. By trying to teach procedures *too much*, teachers begin to appreciate the amount of emphasis procedures need.

Procedures Are the Railroad Tracks — Content Is the Train

I used to try to drag my "trainful" of brilliant lessons along bumpy terrain, uphill both ways. Once I clearly laid down the "railroad tracks" of procedure, the "train" of content ran much more smoothly in the direction I wanted. Consequently, I learned to start the process of teaching procedures on the first day of school; consistent maintenance and "polishing" were essential throughout the year.

A Closer Look

> The clarity of the "tracks" of procedure will determine the direction —and the speed! — of the "train" of content.

When Mrs. Meanswell assumes that her kids are supposed to already know most of the class procedures and routines, or if she is so overwhelmed by the amount of content she is supposed to cover, she may fall into the trap of giving only a quick, cursory overview of procedures. Bad move. The clarity of the "tracks" of procedure will determine the direction — and the speed! — of the "train" of content.

Because of this, procedures come *before* content. And in that sense, they need to be given more priority than content. Additionally, timing is paramount. Mrs. Allgood tends to address procedures *before* disruptions occur, trying to "head problems off at the pass." Mrs. Meanswell tends to address procedures *in response* to disruptions, once the chaos has ensued.

Each procedure needs to be learned, so each needs to be taught. Though it may seem overwhelming to have to teach all of these, most of them are simple and don't take long to establish. Others don't need to be emphasized in the first few days. We should put our attention first on the key procedures that will establish order and focus, and follow up later with the rest. Generally speaking,

Bright Ideas

What Procedures Do We Need?

Below is a partial list of areas where procedures are typically used in K-12 classrooms.

Beginning class

- ▲ Students entering the classroom
- ▲ Using cubbies
- ▲ Tardies
- ▲ Absent excused
- ▲ Absent unexcused
- ▲ Absent students making up work
- ▲ Starting the lesson
- ▲ Turning in homework

During class

- ▲ Getting student attention
- ▲ Listening to P.A. announcements
- ▲ Passing out papers
- ▲ Headings on papers
- ▲ Getting student attention
- ▲ Using the bathroom
- ▲ Using the water fountain
- ▲ Going to lockers
- ▲ Checking out books to students
- ▲ Passing out classroom supplies
- ▲ Using classroom supplies
- ▲ Collecting classroom supplies
- ▲ Turning in class work
- ▲ How students ask for help
- ▲ Checking for understanding
- ▲ Sending students to the office

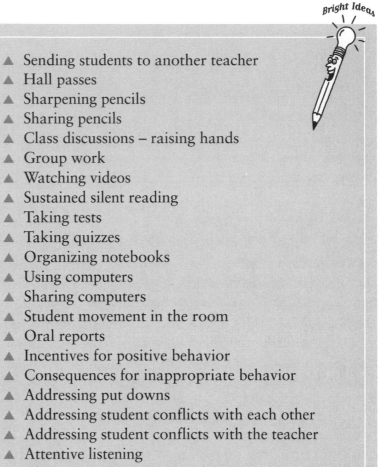

- ▲ Sending students to another teacher
- ▲ Hall passes
- ▲ Sharpening pencils
- ▲ Sharing pencils
- ▲ Class discussions – raising hands
- ▲ Group work
- ▲ Watching videos
- ▲ Sustained silent reading
- ▲ Taking tests
- ▲ Taking quizzes
- ▲ Organizing notebooks
- ▲ Using computers
- ▲ Sharing computers
- ▲ Student movement in the room
- ▲ Oral reports
- ▲ Incentives for positive behavior
- ▲ Consequences for inappropriate behavior
- ▲ Addressing put downs
- ▲ Addressing student conflicts with each other
- ▲ Addressing student conflicts with the teacher
- ▲ Attentive listening
- ▲ Classroom community circles

Special situations

- ▲ Fire drills
- ▲ Field trips
- ▲ Sitting in the auditorium
- ▲ Taking students to the library or computer lab
- ▲ Guest speakers
- ▲ Parent/guardian volunteers in the classroom

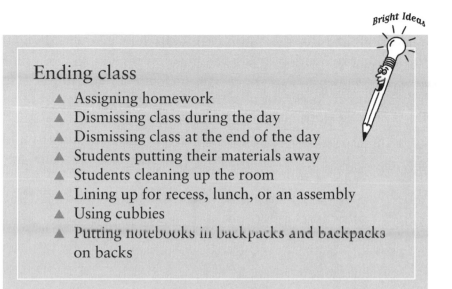

Ending class

- ▲ Assigning homework
- ▲ Dismissing class during the day
- ▲ Dismissing class at the end of the day
- ▲ Students putting their materials away
- ▲ Students cleaning up the room
- ▲ Lining up for recess, lunch, or an assembly
- ▲ Using cubbies
- ▲ Putting notebooks in backpacks and backpacks on backs

students' entering and leaving the classroom, starting class, and getting student attention are the primary procedures to start with. We can add the others systematically in the first few weeks. Check Chapter 10, "Getting Ready," for a "Before-School-Checklist" that can help with organization before school starts.

Mrs. Allgood addresses procedures before disruptions; Mrs. Meanwell addresses them afterward.

How Do I Teach Procedures?

Procedures, like behavior, are taught in the same ways that content is taught. Teaching is teaching and learning is learning, no matter whether we are teaching calculus, singing, foul shooting, lining up for recess, or appropriate behavior during an assembly. The components are still the same. Addressing students' learning styles — visual, auditory, and kinesthetic — can make a big difference. Teachers need to break things into parts, teach the parts and connect them. For example, most students are exposed to the quadratic equation in math class in the 8th or 9th grade. In actuality, they start learning it in kindergarten. Their learning begins with the number line, and moves through addition, subtraction, mul-

A Closer Look

Each procedure needs to be learned, so each needs to be taught.

tiplication, and division, until eventually they can wrestle with the quadratic equation. It is a complex lesson, taking about nine or ten years to implement. In a similar way, in teaching procedures, we need to find a first step that is small enough to allow our students to "get on the escalator." Once that step is established, we can continue to add steps that are appropriately challenging for our students' abilities.

To summarize, there are several steps to teaching procedures effectively:

▲ Determine what procedures are needed
▲ Break them into simple steps
▲ Teach them visually, orally, and/or kinesthetically
▲ Check for understanding
▲ Practice them
▲ Reinforce them
▲ Periodically review them

This process is helped if we assume that students want to succeed, and that procedures are the road map for that success.

Below are four examples for teaching or re-establishing procedures that illustrate different ways to do it.

1. Practicing procedures: group work

If Mrs. Meanswell were to ask her students on the first day of school to "get into groups of four and discuss the story that I just read," she'd more likely than not have total chaos. Group work is a complex task and needs to be taught. In fact, group work is so multi-faceted, most adults in the workplace are still learning it, even though they've been doing it for years. Human Resources Departments of major corporations have reported that many of their employees have a hard time working in teams.

They should watch Mrs. Allgood. By the time her students are ready to practice group work — "working in groups of four" — she has already completed several steps.

First, she determined what the students needed to be taught about the procedure of group work. Her partial list included how to:

- ▲ Move their belongings
- ▲ Move their desks
- ▲ Move their bodies
- ▲ Know where to sit, and with whom
- ▲ Interact with the other moving bodies in the room
- ▲ Listen to the teacher once they are in groups
- ▲ Take turns discussing and staying on task
- ▲ Record responses
- ▲ Encourage each other to participate
- ▲ Elicit full and sincere responses
- ▲ Respect each other's opinion
- ▲ Report out results
- ▲ Listen to others report out
- ▲ Take notes on others reporting out
- ▲ Thank and appreciate their group members
- ▲ Move their belongings back
- ▲ Move their bodies back
- ▲ Move their desks back
- ▲ Refocus their attention once they are moved back

Mrs. Allgood says

Procedures, like behavior, are taught in the same ways that content is taught.

Before tackling "working in groups of four," she drilled her class on working in pairs. She focused on how she wants students to talk with each other, both in terms of describing and practicing the procedure, and in building student accountability for participation in groups. Now, the well-oiled "working in pairs" class is ready.

Mrs. Allgood breaks the new procedure into parts. The first part is getting students into groups. On the overhead projector is depicted an aerial view of the classroom, showing all the desks labeled with students' names and gathered into groups of four with the corners touching. She tells the students to get into their groups according to the "map." She times them. Once they are in groups, she debriefs students on the "lesson" by noting how long it took and giving any commendations and recommendations. "Excellent work, class. It took you forty-five seconds, which is good for a first try. There were two students bumping elbows too much, and one group didn't have their desks touching…"

Then the room is rearranged into its original configuration, and Mrs. Allgood asks the students to try the grouping procedure again. This time she offers them an incentive as a class. "I know you all want extra time today to work on your projects. We'll be practicing getting into groups several times. Each time you can get into groups in fifteen seconds or less without pushing and shoving and with the corners of your desks touching, I'll give you an extra minute and a half at the end of class to work on your projects."

They practice getting in and out of groups several times. Once she feels that the students are getting the procedure, she will "lightly season" the lesson with content. But the procedure is still paramount. Whenever she debriefs the students' group lessons, she always talks about the procedure of group work first, before discussing whatever topic the students talked about.

> *Mrs. Allgood says*
>
> Once we feel that our students are getting the procedure, we can "lightly season" the lesson with content.

This policy that "procedure precedes content" is one element of invisible management, something Mrs. Allgood does consistently. During a discussion, she'll say, "Yes Sally. Thank you for raising your hand (procedure). What is your comment (content)?" Or, "Thank you, class, for being so quiet while José was speaking (procedure). Let's look at his idea… (content)." As Mrs. Allgood focuses on procedures first, she is "polishing the railroad tracks" to allow for the content to flow smoothly.

2. Reviewing procedures regularly

Mrs. Allgood and Mrs. Meanswell each have the same ten-day lesson that involves daily group work toward completion of a project. Each class goes smoothly for the first six days. Then on the seventh day, for no obvious reason, Mrs. Allgood takes three minutes at the start of the lesson to review the procedure for group work. She asks students to clarify their roles and comment on positive things that are working. The lesson ensues, and once again things go smoothly.

In the other classroom, however, Mrs. Meanswell follows the same schedule as in the previous six days and has the students go straight into their groups. Chaos ensues. Disorder, jostling, off-task chatter, loud noises, complaints! Kids get out of their seats *en masse*.

After the lesson Mrs. Meanswell thinks, "I don't understand it. They've been so good for the last six days. It must have been something with the weather, or with their astrological signs, or a weird biochemical aberration…" The next day, or later that day, depending on the grade that's being taught, she has to do her twenty-minute "Sermon on the Mount" — thou shalt not disrupt class, thou shalt respect each other and thou shalt listen to the teacher…" She has to make phone calls to parents and guardians, keep kids after school, basically try to stuff the mushroom cloud back into the canister, all because she didn't spend three minutes at the start of class polishing and maintaining her "railroad tracks."

Did she miss something? Nothing obvious. Effective managers have a sixth sense of knowing when "the natives are about to get restless." Mrs. Allgood simply "knew" that it was time to polish the tracks, even though there was no obvious evidence that the kids were about to act out.

Because none of us has a perfectly developed sixth sense, it makes sense to err on the side of caution. When in doubt, we can take two or three minutes to go over procedural expectations. In the above example Mrs. Allgood reviewed the procedure for group work. She could have used several procedures, such as:

▲ Reminding students of the written directions for the procedure and key points to remember
▲ Informally or formally quizzing students on the procedure (Question 1, multiple choice: "When I ask you to open your books to page 27, you should A)…)

▲ Asking students to recite key steps in the procedure to each other

▲ Asking students to repeat the procedures back to the teacher

▲ Asking students to reflect (out loud or in writing) on the process – what is working, what needs improvement or

▲ Implementing a fishbowl model, whereby a group of students simulates the desired procedure while the rest of the class watches, takes notes, and reviews afterward

The more complex the procedure, the more the students need to focus kinesthetically and visually (not just verbally) in the review. An example might be having the kids practice lining up for recess, or practice setting up and cleaning up labs.

Whatever way we choose to remind students of the appropriate procedures, it makes sense to do it regularly, *before* the students act out.

3. Two procedures per lesson

Research once done on middle school students suggested that more could spell the word "Budweiser" than the word "Eisenhower." My belief is that even if the students had the same number of minutes of exposure to both words over the course of a school year, they would still be able to spell "Budweiser" better. That's because they get Eisenhower once, in a two or three week block called "WWII and the fifties." It's like asking kids to learn content by going through a cave with a flashlight: they don't know Eisenhower is coming, and they don't think about him when he's gone. On the other hand, kids are exposed to Budweiser in 15- and 30-second spots throughout the year. Let's take advantage of "the Budweiser Approach" in teaching and maintaining procedures and routines.

When I taught one class per day of P.E. in an alternative school for at-risk high school students, we had a simple routine. We would meet in my classroom to start the class, and then we would migrate to either the field or the gym (my students didn't change clothes for P.E.). Every day I would take attendance, and then I would make some simple announcements. Here is a typical one:

"Class, yesterday we went up to the gym to play volleyball. I want to commend you on how well you walked through the halls. There was no banging of the lockers and nobody stuck their head in the doors of classes that were in session. As a group you all walked quietly and efficiently to the gym. That was wonderful. Today, we will be playing volleyball again, and I want to remind you that volleyballs are for hands only. Any questions? No? Let's go."

I had about six key procedures for volleyball, one of which was that they were for hands only. If I didn't mention "hands only" at least once every three days, by the fourth day balls would be kicked all over the gym, with offending students looking at me with that classic duck-and-cover look on their faces — "What? I didn't know. You never said. Huh?"

My using little spot-check "Budweisers" throughout the school year was so successful in cutting down chaos that I suggest it to all teachers. Every class period or lesson, try consciously to teach at least two procedures — regardless of what the lesson is. This entails more than simply thanking a student for speaking in a nice loud voice. Teachers can mix up modalities, rotating between auditory, visual, and kinesthetic reminders. Although I had to teach the procedures in the beginning of P.E. class to avoid yelling procedures across the field, classroom teachers don't necessarily need to. Choose appropriate points in each class or lesson.

Every class period or lesson, try consciously to teach at least two procedures

By teaching a minimum of two procedures per class for secondary teachers, or per lesson for elementary teachers, not only will classes run more smoothly and kids be able to learn content faster, teachers will consciously exercise their muscles of inner authority, and the dividends will pay off down the line in all aspects of their teaching.

4. Rubrics for procedures

A rubric strategy will work for any elementary or secondary classroom requirement that can be modeled, drawn, photographed or otherwise illustrated. For example, elementary students can be shown five different qualities of lining up. A very poor line would be a "one"; an excellent line would be a "five." Students need to have a "five" before they are ready to leave the classroom. With sufficient modeling, they will tend to self-monitor their lines by referencing the quality of the line to a number: "C'mon everybody, we look like a three!" They'll need little or no direction from the teacher.

To make it even clearer, a teacher can take pictures of the students in the five different "lineups," number the pictures, and then put them over the door to the classroom. Students can then reference the pictures as they form their lines. All the teacher has to do is stand under the door facing the kids and hold up her fingers to correspond to the quality of the line. When she holds up five fingers, the class is ready to go.

Another example involves getting students to straighten desks and clean the room before they are dismissed. The teacher can provide a rubric for a clean and straightened room. The kids know that unless the room is a "five" they won't be dismissed. Pictures of the room can be taken in various stages of cleanliness. Student readiness also can be included in the pictures; for example, even if all the desks are lined up and the paper is thrown out, backpacks must be on the floor and students seated before the room is a "five." Again, the students will self-monitor, talking among themselves rather than arguing with the teacher. And they will tend to be much more efficient.

The applications of rubrics for procedures are many, including lab or art set up and clean up, P.E. activities, and forming groups. In addition to posting photographs, the teacher can put them onto overheads and display them in front of the room when appropriate.

Things To Do

Getting the class quiet

An effective learning environment does not *always* have to be "pin-drop" quiet for at least two reasons. First, for student brains to grow, active learning needs to take place, which often involves talking and/or moving. Second, along with content, we also teach social skills, so students need time in class where talking is "legal."

Conversely, student silence often *is* a necessary ingredient for successful learning. Below are some procedures that help to get students quiet in those "rare" moments when they are clearly talking out of turn. Of course, like all procedures, these must be taught, practiced, and reviewed to be successful.

Students entering the classroom

If our kids enter our classroom in a rowdy, disruptive manner, then during class we can have them practice the procedure for entering the classroom. We can review the correct procedure, then direct students to pick up their belongings and leave the classroom, wait for our signal, and walk back into the room as if the class was about to start. We can check for understanding by calling on students to describe the procedure. We can give the kids a quiz on the

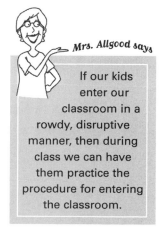

Wise Apple Advice

A teacher can take pictures of the students in the five different "lineups," number the pictures, and then put them over the door to the classroom. Students can then reference the pictures as they form their lines.

Mrs. Allgood says

If our kids enter our classroom in a rowdy, disruptive manner, then during class we can have them practice the procedure for entering the classroom.

proper way to enter the classroom. We can also let them know when they do a good job. These approaches will work with kids K-12. Once they learn the procedure, classes consistently will start more smoothly.

Class complaints

When I taught social studies to at-risk high school kids, we'd often play games on Fridays. Therefore, I established a procedure for those Fridays when, for whatever reason, we didn't play a game. At the start of class, I would announce that we wouldn't be having a game, and then I implemented our procedure — called "Complaining out loud for up to three seconds in a G-rated manner." First I counted out loud to three, then put my hand to my ear and listened to three seconds of complaining, moaning, and whining. When I'd give the stop signal, by moving my hand across my neck, the complaining would cease. All they needed was for me to acknowledge their dissatisfaction; after that, I'd proceed to teach a much more relaxed and focused group of students.

A Closer Look

When students' dissatisfaction is acknowledged, they tend to relax and focus on the lesson at hand.

Jokes and laughter

Many teachers find that when they tell a joke or a funny story, the kids seem to think that they are allowed to take several minutes to indulge in jokes of their own. One solution is to have the students practice the procedure for responding to jokes. The teacher can clarify that it's totally acceptable to laugh and feel good, but that they need to get back on task when she gives a special "post-laugh" hand signal. After they practice responding to the signal, they'll be much more likely to get back on-task faster in the future.

Tattling

Some of our students, especially in elementary school, are chronic tattlers. It's often not enough to simply tell them not to complain about each other. We need to teach them appropriate alternatives. For example, we can establish a procedure during classroom community circles to address student conflicts and concerns. We can ask students to role-play appropriate ways to address conflicts. We can teach them to differentiate between that which is their business and that which is gossip. Or between that which is a safety issue, either physically or emotionally, and that which is not. We can also create a suggestion box where students can place their tattles. This will allow the tattlers to get their concerns off their chests without disrupting class.

Move, move, move!

We can use movement and gestures to keep kids interested — and quiet. **Proximity** helps keep them focused. In class discussions, we can **go near** inattentive students when we are talking. This offers them a gentle reminder to refocus their attention. We can **go away** from students when they are contributing during a class discussion. This puts distance between the student and ourselves, compelling him to speak louder so we can hear him. Plus, by keeping our distance, we place the whole class in front of us, and we put the majority of the students between the student who is talking and ourselves. This means that if paper airplanes begin to fly, at least we can see the source.

Mrs. Allgood says

Go near students when we are talking, and away from them when they are contributing out loud.

Pause

We can stop talking to let students know they are interrupting. We can pause in our "proximity procedure" when we are near disruptive students long enough that they don't just pause — they stop.

Eye contact

This works well when trying to get student attention. For some reason, students cannot make eye contact with the teacher and talk to their neighbor at the same time. Asking students to look at the teacher tends to quiet them immediately. Please note: there are some cultural differences among students that affect this strategy. Some students are raised to believe that it is disrespectful to look the teacher in the eye, especially when in a private conversation. In this case, learn about the customs of students in the class, and if necessary, develop specific, appropriate alternatives.

Greet students at the door

This aids students' perception that the classroom is a safe and warm environment with a teacher who cares enough to show personal regard for them. They tend to relax, follow directions, and listen respectfully in this environment. If greeting our students is a logistical challenge, eye contact at or near the start of class is a helpful substitute.

Say students' names

This is more effective in getting student attention than "class" or "settle down." If Sally is talking, saying Mark's name will often quiet Sally as well.

Use a firm yet soft voice

When holding our ground effectively with students, our firm yet soft voice can communicate that there is no wiggle room for them. There is no rancor or sarcasm or put-downs in our voice, but there is also no self-apology either. It is clear and direct.

Vary tone and volume

It helps to speak with, not at students. Sometimes when teachers speak in a monotone, they edit out all indicators of enthusiasm for what they're talking about. Students pick up on this, get bored, feel unappreciated, and begin to act out.

Seating arrangement

Many new teachers, especially at the elementary level, seem to think that putting students in rows is not only politically incorrect, but also could be psychologically damaging. I don't want to debate the subtle underpinnings here. Suffice it to say that if kids are acting out while sitting in groups or circles, rows will tend to quiet them down and focus them up front. And sometimes that quiet focus matters more than anything else. It establishes a safe, directed environment with the teacher in charge. So at least as a temporary measure, let's not hesitate to go for it. Seating arrangement is discussed in more detail in Chapter 10 "Getting Ready."

Mrs. Allgood says

> If kids are acting out while sitting in groups or circles, rows will tend to quiet them down and focus them up front.

Count backwards from 20 to 1

Whatever number we have come to when the class is totally quiet equals the number of points (or marbles in a jar) that the class gets toward a group privilege. This can be extra time to focus on their projects, or a pre-approved activity of their choice, such as a short video, ten minutes extra recess, or the chance to do homework during class.

Hold up a timer

The number of seconds that elapse while we wait can be removed from a pre-set group reward. Or, we can establish a maximum amount of acceptable "settle-down time." If the students "beat the clock" throughout a given time period — twice a day for primary, once a day for upper elementary, twice a week for middle school, once a week for high school — they receive a class reward. Classroom management consultant Fred Jones refers to this as PAT: Preferred Activity Time. It's an incentive that students earn by being efficient and productive. If the incentive we give them is an enjoyable, educational activity we want them to do anyway, then everybody wins.

Hold up a hand

When students see our raised hand, they know to stop talking and to raise their hands, thus helping signal others to be quiet as well.

Use class coupons

Try strips of gold paper that say "positive performance coupon" with a blank line for a student's name. When a student is on task, we quietly give him a coupon. He then knows to print his name on it, and silently place it in a fishbowl in the front of the room. At the end of the day or week, the fishbowl is used for raffle awards determined by the teacher.

Get full silence before continuing

When we "talk over" chattering students, not only do they get the message that they don't need to be completely quiet, but also many students will not hear what we say. This will lead to more of the chaos that we're trying to avoid in the first place. Granted, in the beginning it might seem as if we have to wait forever. But by being patient, and by using one or more of the suggestions in this chapter, things will tend to turn around quickly.

Mrs. Allgood says

Pick a song that our students like — and that we can live with! — and designate it as the signal for a given transition.

Use music for transitions

A first grade art teacher plays the song "Whistle While You Work," signaling students to begin cleaning up. When the song is over, the room is clean, the supplies are put away, and the students are seated in circle for the closure activity. The students are so used to the procedure that one day when the teacher forgot the music and asked the students to clean up, they all complained, "Where's the song?"

This procedure works for any grade level. We should pick a song that our students like — and that we can live with! — and designate it as the signal for a given transition. If the transition is to last thirty seconds, then we should play only the last thirty seconds of the song. We can use different songs for different standard transitions. We can also give incentives if all students have completed a given transition by the time the song is over.

Playing fast-paced music can speed up transition time. Many restaurants play fast-paced music in the background to make their customers unconsciously eat faster, thereby increasing the number of patrons per day.

Use a sound signal to get student attention

Squeaky toys, electronic sounds — anything that can be bought at a toy store — can work well to get student attention. Sounds, which are predominantly right-brain oriented, tend to cut through the students' "left-brain chatter" much better than a teacher's voice. Consultant Rick Morris suggests using several different sounds, with each one geared toward a specific class procedure. For example, for third graders he uses a train whistle to get students to line up, and a hotel bell to let group leaders know to come up and collect handouts to distribute to their group members.

Have students use hand signals

Also from Rick Morris, this strategy has proven quite useful, especially in elementary and middle schools. If a student has a **question**, he holds a fist in the air with pinky extended — sign language for "I," as in "I have a question." If a student wants to **answer** a question, he holds his fist in the air with thumb pointing up — sign language for "A," as in "I have an answer." If a student has a **comment**, he holds his hand up in the form of the letter "C." If a student needs to use the **bathroom**, he holds up his hand with the middle finger crossed over the forefinger — "R," for restroom.

By using these hand signals, the teacher receives more information about what kind of comments are hiding behind the raised hands of her students. Students feel safer asking questions, because they know the teacher won't call on them unless it's an appropriate time to address questions. Plus, students will no longer interrupt class to ask permission to use the bathroom.

If a student is disruptive, either by butting into our private conversation with another student, or by doing the, "Oh-oh-oh, call on me call on me" raised hand strategy, another signal we can use is the extended index finger. When we hold out it up at about a 45-degree angle, we signal the student that we acknowledge his desire for our attention, and we'll address his issue shortly. He can then put his hand down or back away from our private conversation, without worrying that no one will acknowledge his life-or-death need to tell us a story about a cool insect he saw this morning.

A Closer Look

By using hand signals, the teacher receives more information about what kind of comments are hiding behind the raised hands of her students.

Directions, questions

There is an art to giving directions, as well as asking questions. As we grow in "teacher presence," many of the strategies below naturally occur. Nonetheless, it helps to lay down our own "tracks."

Be clear in directions and questions

When Mrs. Meanswell asks, "Does everyone have a copy?" she'll get a chorus of yeses, but not from the students who need one. As an alternative, she can ask, "Who needs one?" Instead of, "Would you like to read now?" she can say, "We're going to read now," or better yet, "Please take out your books and open to page twenty-seven."

I remember an incident from my first year as a substitute teacher that would have been quite comical if it weren't so painful to watch. I was observing a student teacher, who at one point asked the students: "Would you like to do some reading now?" As soon as the words left her mouth, I knew she was in trouble. The students naturally responded with, "No." Then she said, "I really think it would be a good idea if we read now," and later, "Could we please read now?" Of course, the students responded each time with, "No." Eventually she got them to open their books and begin reading, but not without a struggle.

A note on the word "please"

Many teachers have asked me if I think it's okay to use the word "please" in giving directions. My answer? Absolutely, as long as it is spoken as a statement, rather than a question. Correctly imparted, "please" simply communicates respect, rather than loopholes, self-apology, or weakness.

The lack of student questions does not mean that they understand

It's a good practice to ask specific students to repeat back to us what we've said — regardless of whether it's about procedure, behavior, or content — to make sure that everyone is on the same page. One way is to ask reluctant learner Morgan to listen to and evaluate Maria's summary of the procedure. Morgan becomes a class consultant and learns the procedure. Maria gets a chance to show off her knowledge. Other students are on their toes in case they get called on next.

Mrs. Allgood says

Correctly imparted, "please" simply communicates respect, rather than loopholes, self-apology, or weakness.

It's also helpful to write down our directions on an overhead, on the board, on a flip chart, or on a handout. We can periodically and systematically refer to the written directions. Our visual learners will love us for it. For complex procedures, our students can do several "walk-throughs" before they do the actual activity.

For complex procedures, break directions into digestible chunks

Often teachers try to give all the directions to a complex procedure beforehand, and students end up lost. It makes more sense to give the students only what they need to know first, and add to the procedure as they are ready for more. Imagine following a complicated cooking procedure and being allowed to look at the recipe only once before starting.

For simple procedures in group work, give directions beforehand

By doing this we eliminate the need to silence the class right after they form their groups. Plus, when students are in groups facing each other, their attention naturally goes in the direction of their group members, making it harder for them to focus on our directions. As above, if group-work directions are detailed, give chunks at appropriate intervals.

Also, when possible, groups can be dissolved before having them report their findings to the class. This is so they'll have an easier time paying attention to each student speaker.

Mrs. Allgood says

During student presentations, have students listen for key words or phrases that they can report on afterward.

Helping group presentations succeed

Limit the number of group presentations per lesson – too many will lead to restlessness and acting out. It's also helpful to consistently reinforce appropriate audience behavior throughout any lesson where students need to listen to each other. We can remind students what's appropriate, thank them when they listen attentively, and stop them in their tracks if they don't. One procedure I like to use goes like this: I remind students to listen with their eyes (on the speaker), mouths (closed), hands (quiet), as well as with their ears. I often have students listen for key words or phrases that they can report on afterward. This builds in accountability and helps develop analytical thinking skills. Finally, I ensure that whenever a student speaker is finished, all class members applaud. Applause serves several purposes. First, it makes the speaker feel good. Second, it focuses the class together as a group. And third, it energizes students, helping them refocus for the next speaker.

In many classes, students will tend to applaud for the first student speaker, and then "space out" for the remaining speakers. It's one of my pet peeves. I always make it a point to see that all my students applaud each time; otherwise what is intended to be a positive community-building experience can come across as a put-down for a given speaker.

Bathroom procedure

Mrs. Allgood says

Students who don't use their bathroom passes receive a reimbursement, such as extra credit.

Primarily for secondary classes: teachers give students a certain number of non-transferable bathroom passes per semester — three or four is the usual number. If a student has used all his passes, then each subsequent time he needs to use the bathroom, he owes the teacher time after class, whether during lunch, recess, or whenever is most convenient for the teacher. Students who don't use their bathroom passes receive a reimbursement, such as extra credit. Or the whole class can "cash in" their bathroom passes for something special. Some teachers report that when the class has the opportunity to "buy" something with their unused bathroom passes, the peer pressure to keep kids from using the bathroom generally ensures that kids go only when they really need to.

9

CONSISTENCY

Mrs. Meanswell:	Mark, didn't you promise to behave?
Mark:	Yes.
Mrs. Meanswell:	And didn't I promise you there'd be a consequence if you didn't?
Mark:	Yes, but since I broke my promise, I don't expect you to keep yours.

Test Wednesday!

solve for X

$$\sqrt{2 + Y(27 - X^2)} = \frac{Y}{X^3}$$

Do problems 1-23

pgs. 115 - 120

I MEET WITH STUDENT LAWYERS ON FRIDAYS AT 4:30

HERMANSEN

T HERE'S AN OLD SAYING: "Once the camel gets its nose in the tent, the rest of the animal is sure to follow." Another more modern version is, "Give a mouse a cookie and he wants a glass of milk." Our inconsistency can send our class mixed messages, and those messages can invite camels into the tent for afternoon tea — and students into inappropriate behavior. Since we are the authors of what happens in the classroom, students follow our lead — and they behave in ways we unconsciously allow. The trick is to get conscious — and consistent.

In March a couple of years ago, I began mentoring a first-year fifth-grade teacher. She had been teaching since the beginning of the school year, and was struggling.

I sat in the back of the room while she taught, and in ten minutes I wrote down twenty-five suggestions. Honestly, among her repertoire, I didn't see much she should continue to do. Transitions seemed to elongate and blend into one another so that there really wasn't a whole lot of teaching going on between them. The kids interrupted constantly, redirecting the flow of the class easily and often. The "camel"

A Closer Look

We are the authors of what happens in the classroom. Students follow our lead and behave in ways that we unconsciously allow.

105

of student interruption hadn't just gotten its nose in the tent, it was reclining on a chaise lounge.

As I sat looking at my notes, I knew that if I shared my twenty-five suggestions with this teacher in our first post-observation meeting, I was toast. Not only would she resist any of my suggestions, she would probably sever what few ties we had to each other. Just as students balk when they receive their essays back with twenty-five suggestions in red ink, so do teachers balk when they are already overwhelmed and then get a bunch of ideas thrown at them.

I realized that I needed to pare down my ideas to no more than a few. This teacher needed a manageable handful of threads to follow, threads that would anchor her to some basic strategies for classroom survival. I came up with three. I introduced them one at a time over a period of weeks, which allowed her to start experiencing success in her classroom. All three ideas, as it turns out, have three things in common. Each is:

▲ Immediately applicable to all K-12 teachers
▲ Focused on teacher consistency
▲ Practical and doable

All the other aspects of good teaching — holding our ground, effective lesson design, teaching procedures — are supported by these three suggestions, which are described below. Don't be fooled by their simplicity; consistency takes a lot of focus and practice before it becomes second nature. If she works hard at it, Mrs. Meanswell can discover a new teaching "muscle," one that will keep the wildlife outdoors.

1. Hand and Mouth Dis-ease

Just about every teacher has a procedure in place where students are asked to raise their hands and be called on before they speak. In all my years as a mentor, I have never seen any teacher be absolutely consistent with this simple procedure. Students flow through the inconsistencies like water. Maria will raise her hand and call out the right answer. Manny will yell out the right answer without bothering to raise his hand. Even Mrs. Allgood isn't absolutely consistent in this. After years of practice, she can proudly state that about ninety-eight percent of the time, she is aware when she is being inconsistent.

Mrs. Allgood says

When students call out, we need to honor the procedure rather than the content.

The solution involves bringing awareness to the procedure and practicing being consistent. When students call out, we need to honor the procedure rather than the content. In Manny's case, we can respond with something like, "That's a great answer, Manny. Could you please raise your hand, let me call on you, and then you can repeat it so the whole class can hear you."

Especially if Manny is normally a reluctant participant, it can be a temptation to acknowledge his good answers even when they are called out of turn. But giving in will send a mixed message to students about procedures, penalize those who don't call out, and ultimately lead to adding the camel's name to the mailbox.

A clear hand-raising procedure is one of the hardest things for teachers to enforce consistently. It takes practice and self-discipline, but it makes a huge difference in the noise level in the classroom. For the struggling fifth-grade teacher, this may well have been the most valuable tip she focused on. I suggested that when she woke up in the morning, rather than thinking, "I'm going to cover such-and-such content today," or "Today, I'm going to be a better classroom manager," think instead, "Today, I will be more consistent about hand raising than I was yesterday." I gave her a clip-art picture of a hand and she posted it on the back wall where she could easily see it. The students asked her what the hand was for, and she replied, "To help me be consistent in asking you to raise your hands to be called on." Two stu-

I suggested that when she woke up in the morning, rather than thinking, "I'm going to cover such-and-such content today," she should think instead, "Today, I will be more consistent about hand raising than I was yesterday."

dents naturally asked, "Can we help?" — so then she had the "hand police" working on her side. She gave them a special hand signal to remind her when she was inconsistent. Ultimately, the awareness and the "muscle" of consistency inside her began to grow. By focusing on one area, she become much more conscious of the whole realm of procedures and consistency, and this ultimately began to spill into other key areas of her teaching.

2. Arguing with the Ref

Have you ever come back to your car during a shopping spree to put money in the meter, only to discover that you're too late, and there's already a ticket on your windshield? At that point you think to yourself that you might as well not move your car or put money in the meter. Simply keep the ticket on the windshield, and go back to shopping. No parking officer is going to give you *two* tickets.

In a similar way, students often feel that once they've received a consequence from us, all bets are off. They figure there's no way we're going to give them a second consequence for arguing; they've already hit bottom, so they have every right to argue about it. This "arguing with the ref" applies to all those times when students argue with teacher decisions, and it can drive teachers crazy.

For example, Mark is talking to Susie out of turn. Mrs. Meanswell has warned him several times to no avail. She then tells him that he has to change his seat. Does he pop right up and walk to the new seat, thanking Mrs. Meanswell profusely for teaching him appropriate behavior? Forget about it! Instead, he argues with her. She then "takes the bait" by explaining why Mark needs to change seats, attempting to justify her decision. Or, she doesn't explain, but does end up verbally warning, cajoling, and/or threatening Mark until he takes his sweet time, noisily complaining as he saunters across the room.

In this example, Mrs. Meanswell is the ref and Mark is arguing with her. What she needs to understand and enforce is that his argument is in itself a disruption, deserving a second consequence. The first consequence for talking to Mark is changing his seat. The second consequence for arguing with the ref is something in addition to changing his seat. This second consequence can be determined based on Mrs. Meanswell's existing hierarchy of consequences (see chapter 12 "Rules and Consequences" for possibilities).

Mrs. Allgood addresses student arguing proactively. She establishes the procedures for when a student disagrees with her decisions, and makes it clear that "arguing with the ref" is in itself a misbehavior that will warrant a separate consequence.

Let's look at how she handles Mark's disruption. If Mark disagrees with her decision to change his seat, he holds his hands up to form a "T" (for "talk") — like a time-out signal. She nods to acknowledge the signal, and silently directs him to his new seat. Mark quietly changes seats. Later, they have a private conversation where Mark can voice his protest. If it turns out that Mark has a legitimate point, she thanks him for waiting to talk to her, she changes his seat back, and publicly acknowledges how well Mark followed the procedure for disagreeing with her decision. The whole process with Mark will become a model for all of her students' future behavior.

A Closer Look

Student argument is in itself a disruption, deserving a second consequence.

Whether or not we decide to use the "T" for students to voice their protests (an alternative to the "T" signal is a special "teacher-student" conversation pass, that students pick up at the back of the room and "cash-in" when they want to talk privately with their teacher), we can still benefit from an increased consciousness about "arguing with the ref." The main element is simply to be aware that students do not have the right to protest our decisions whenever they choose. We have the right to table their protests until such a time that twenty or thirty pairs of eyes are not watching the debate.

One benefit to tabling student arguments is that students will often not follow through with their protest, because their original concern was more of an emotional outburst than a logical disagreement.

A Closer Look

> We have the right to table their protests until such a time that twenty or thirty pairs of eyes are not watching the debate.

What about when a student argues on behalf of his friend? His arguing is equally disruptive, and needs to be addressed as such. One strategy is to post a sign on the wall in the front of the room that reads, "I meet with student lawyers on Fridays at 4:30." Whenever a student argues for his friend, the teacher can simply point to the sign, and move on. A similar sign reads, "This is a student-lawyer free zone."

When orchestrating procedures intended to decrease student arguing, our aim is to include all students in the learning process as much as possible, and to avoid student distractions. With more awareness and practice, we will naturally "take the bait" less, and our classroom disruptions will settle down.

3. The Popcorn Effect

Imagine that you're making popcorn on the stove. You've got a pan full of unpopped kernels on low heat with the top off. One kernel pops and flies behind you on the kitchen floor. You turn around and bend down to retrieve it, and by the time you come back to the stove, hundreds of kernels have popped and they are all over the kitchen — because you forgot to put the lid on the skillet.

How does this translate to the classroom?

Get all students actively on-task before having individual conversations with any of them.

A couple of years ago, I observed a middle school P.E. teacher who broke this guideline three times in about twelve seconds. The kids had run a lap and were standing on their numbers on the blacktop. As the teacher was about to announce the basketball activity, Mark raised his hand. The teacher committed her first mistake when she called on him before starting the activity. "I wasn't here yesterday when you gave us our grades," he said. "Could you tell me my grade?"

Her second mistake: "Sure. Come on up." A better answer would have been, "I talk to students about grades on Tuesdays and Thursdays at 3 o'clock. Please see me then." When Mark walked up, the teacher turned her back to the class in order to privately show him his grade. Mistake number three!

> Two seconds after the teacher turned her back, the students were wrestling on the asphalt. Three seconds after that, they were picking up loose pieces of asphalt and throwing them at each other.

I was in the back observing and taking notes. About two seconds after the teacher turned her back, these eighth-graders — with their usual, collective attention span of a gnat — were no longer standing on their numbers. They were wrestling on the asphalt. Three seconds after that, they were no longer just wrestling — they were picking up loose pieces of asphalt and throwing them at each other. Three seconds later, the teacher turned around to see total "popcorn" bedlam. After class, she remarked to me, "These are just bad kids." It was unfortunate that she drew that conclusion from the lesson she taught.

Getting and keeping kids on task without having to constantly put out fires is a tall order for many of us. Keeping the "camel" of student disruption out of the tent begins with two guidelines. First, *minimize* the number and length of private conversations held during class. Otherwise, the kids will receive the message that it's okay to be off-task when the teacher is having a private conversation. Second, *maximize* our opportunities for private conversations, by building in activities where the rest of the class will be focused for at least a few minutes — perhaps a short video or a competition among pairs, something sure to keep them on-task without our constant "shushing."

It can be quite a challenge to hold off responding to individual students' needs. We want to help our students. We want to be fair and kind and caring. Yet when we attend to one student's apparent needs to the neglect of all our other students, trouble is sure

Mrs. Allgood says

Minimize the number and length of private conversations held during class, while maximizing the opportunities for them.

to follow. It can help if we ask ourselves if what the student is asking for is a "need" or a "want." "Does it need to be addressed now, or can I do it later, at a time when I am not on stage with the rest of my students?" Nine times out of ten, the student is expressing a want, and that want can be addressed at a later time.

Other Consistency Keys

As we follow the three threads of consistency outlined above, our effectiveness in all areas of consistency will increase. Other keys to consistency, addressed in various chapters in this book, include:

- ▲ Holding our ground without over-explaining
- ▲ Staying focused on the topic even as students try to change it
- ▲ Teaching and re-teaching procedures
- ▲ Starting and ending class on time
- ▲ Enforcing and following through with consequences
- ▲ Talking with parents/guardians
- ▲ Welcoming and encouraging students

Wise Apple Advice

Relaxing into consistency

Being consistent doesn't mean being a robot or a machine. It arises out of our caring for our students, and caring for their learning. As we combine an open resilient quality with a commitment to teach students content, behavior, and procedures, we naturally become more consistent, without losing our humanity or spontaneity.

10

GETTING READY

> *"Everything should be made as simple as possible, but not simpler."*
>
> — ALBERT EINSTEIN

You must be the new teacher. Here are your room keys,
roll sheet, lesson plans and spit-wad deflector suit.

ONE THING MRS. MEANSWELL won't see when observing Mrs. Allgood is what she does to get ready before she ever gets to the classroom. Her organization and preparation are keys to smooth teaching and smooth management. As a new teacher, or one who is transferring to a new school or district, these are particularly important skills to learn, because there are so many things to do and consider. This chapter lays out much of the nitty-gritty for getting ready before the students arrive, as well as what to do in the first weeks of school. At the end of this chapter is a step-by-step guide called "What to do first?" that ties many key elements together.

What to Do Before School Starts

Suppose it's June and you just got hired at a new school for a new teaching job that begins in August. Whether it's your first job or your tenth, there are certain "before-school preparations" that can help take the edge off those first days and weeks of school:

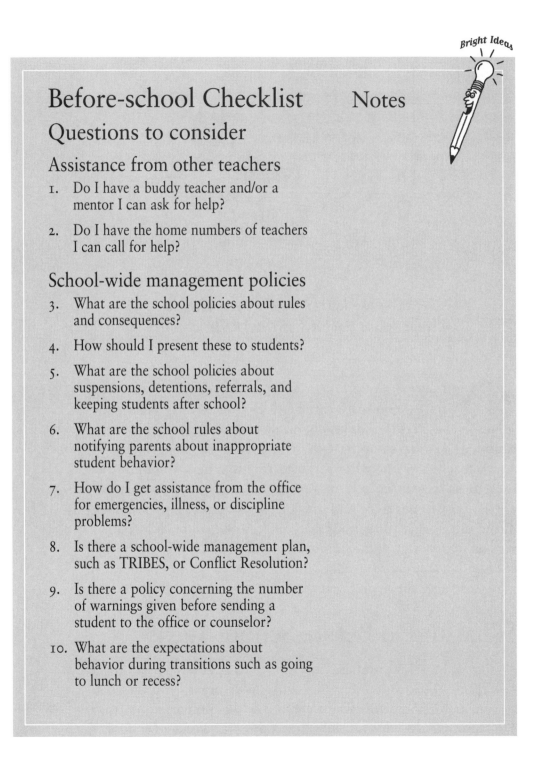

Bright Ideas

Before-school Checklist   Notes
Questions to consider
Assistance from other teachers

1. Do I have a buddy teacher and/or a mentor I can ask for help?

2. Do I have the home numbers of teachers I can call for help?

School-wide management policies

3. What are the school policies about rules and consequences?

4. How should I present these to students?

5. What are the school policies about suspensions, detentions, referrals, and keeping students after school?

6. What are the school rules about notifying parents about inappropriate student behavior?

7. How do I get assistance from the office for emergencies, illness, or discipline problems?

8. Is there a school-wide management plan, such as TRIBES, or Conflict Resolution?

9. Is there a policy concerning the number of warnings given before sending a student to the office or counselor?

10. What are the expectations about behavior during transitions such as going to lunch or recess?

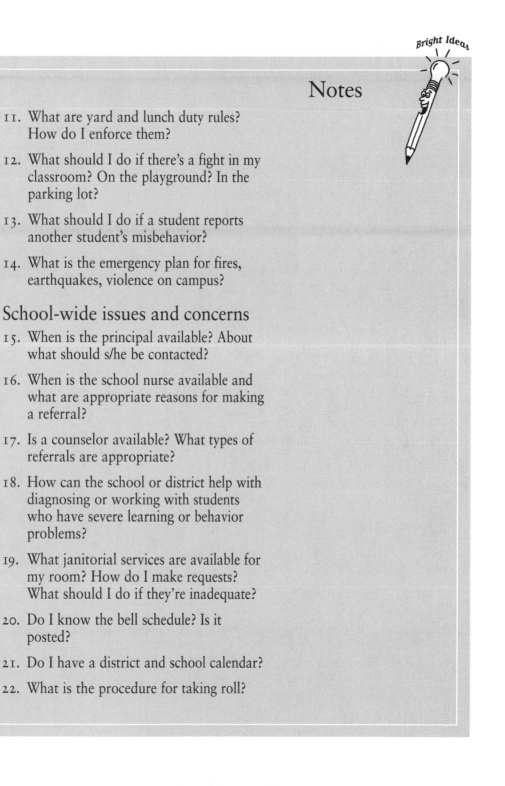

Notes

11. What are yard and lunch duty rules? How do I enforce them?

12. What should I do if there's a fight in my classroom? On the playground? In the parking lot?

13. What should I do if a student reports another student's misbehavior?

14. What is the emergency plan for fires, earthquakes, violence on campus?

School-wide issues and concerns

15. When is the principal available? About what should s/he be contacted?

16. When is the school nurse available and what are appropriate reasons for making a referral?

17. Is a counselor available? What types of referrals are appropriate?

18. How can the school or district help with diagnosing or working with students who have severe learning or behavior problems?

19. What janitorial services are available for my room? How do I make requests? What should I do if they're inadequate?

20. Do I know the bell schedule? Is it posted?

21. Do I have a district and school calendar?

22. What is the procedure for taking roll?

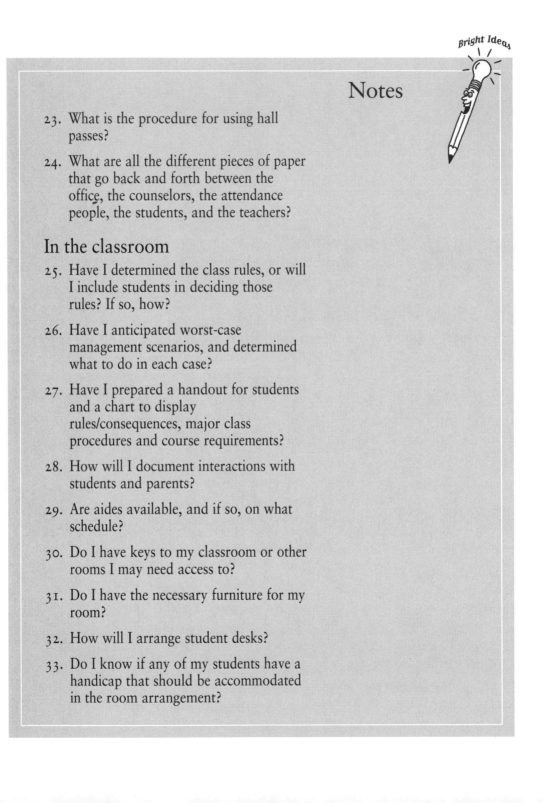

Bright Ideas

Notes

23. What is the procedure for using hall passes?

24. What are all the different pieces of paper that go back and forth between the office, the counselors, the attendance people, the students, and the teachers?

In the classroom

25. Have I determined the class rules, or will I include students in deciding those rules? If so, how?

26. Have I anticipated worst-case management scenarios, and determined what to do in each case?

27. Have I prepared a handout for students and a chart to display rules/consequences, major class procedures and course requirements?

28. How will I document interactions with students and parents?

29. Are aides available, and if so, on what schedule?

30. Do I have keys to my classroom or other rooms I may need access to?

31. Do I have the necessary furniture for my room?

32. How will I arrange student desks?

33. Do I know if any of my students have a handicap that should be accommodated in the room arrangement?

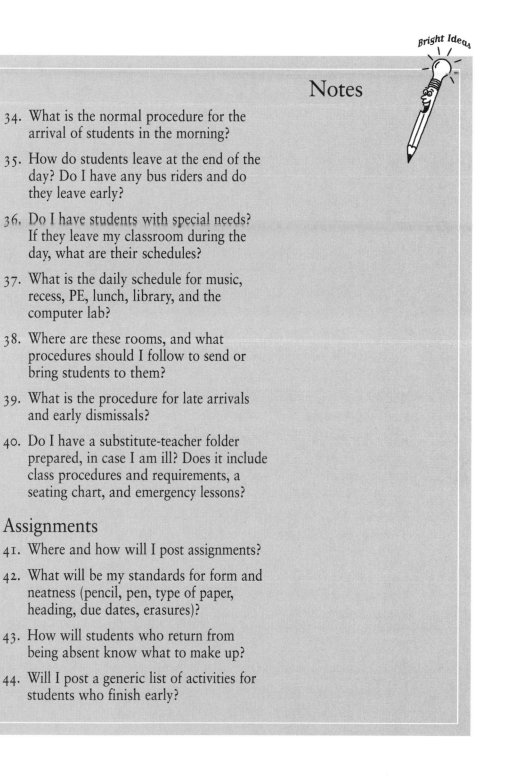

Bright Ideas

Notes

34. What is the normal procedure for the arrival of students in the morning?

35. How do students leave at the end of the day? Do I have any bus riders and do they leave early?

36. Do I have students with special needs? If they leave my classroom during the day, what are their schedules?

37. What is the daily schedule for music, recess, PE, lunch, library, and the computer lab?

38. Where are these rooms, and what procedures should I follow to send or bring students to them?

39. What is the procedure for late arrivals and early dismissals?

40. Do I have a substitute-teacher folder prepared, in case I am ill? Does it include class procedures and requirements, a seating chart, and emergency lessons?

Assignments

41. Where and how will I post assignments?

42. What will be my standards for form and neatness (pencil, pen, type of paper, heading, due dates, erasures)?

43. How will students who return from being absent know what to make up?

44. Will I post a generic list of activities for students who finish early?

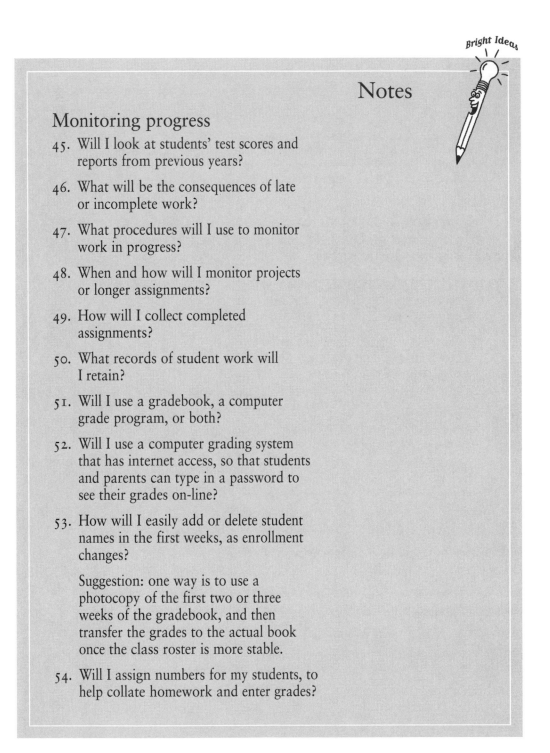

Bright Ideas

Notes

Monitoring progress

45. Will I look at students' test scores and reports from previous years?

46. What will be the consequences of late or incomplete work?

47. What procedures will I use to monitor work in progress?

48. When and how will I monitor projects or longer assignments?

49. How will I collect completed assignments?

50. What records of student work will I retain?

51. Will I use a gradebook, a computer grade program, or both?

52. Will I use a computer grading system that has internet access, so that students and parents can type in a password to see their grades on-line?

53. How will I easily add or delete student names in the first weeks, as enrollment changes?

    Suggestion: one way is to use a photocopy of the first two or three weeks of the gradebook, and then transfer the grades to the actual book once the class roster is more stable.

54. Will I assign numbers for my students, to help collate homework and enter grades?

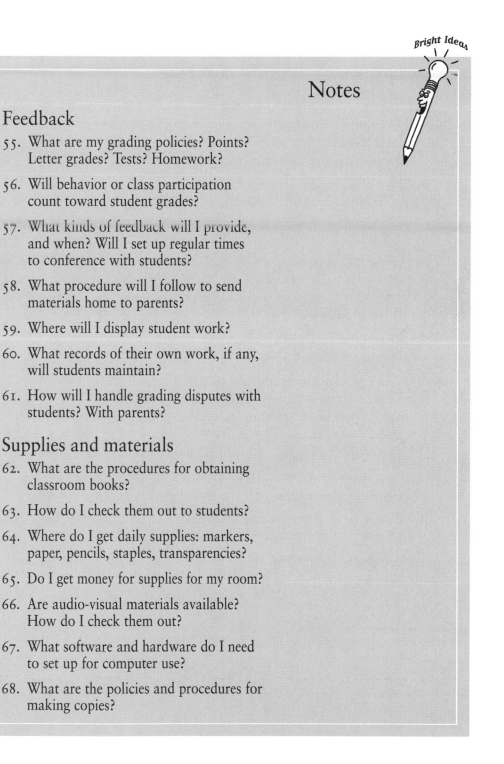

Notes

Feedback

55. What are my grading policies? Points? Letter grades? Tests? Homework?

56. Will behavior or class participation count toward student grades?

57. What kinds of feedback will I provide, and when? Will I set up regular times to conference with students?

58. What procedure will I follow to send materials home to parents?

59. Where will I display student work?

60. What records of their own work, if any, will students maintain?

61. How will I handle grading disputes with students? With parents?

Supplies and materials

62. What are the procedures for obtaining classroom books?

63. How do I check them out to students?

64. Where do I get daily supplies: markers, paper, pencils, staples, transparencies?

65. Do I get money for supplies for my room?

66. Are audio-visual materials available? How do I check them out?

67. What software and hardware do I need to set up for computer use?

68. What are the policies and procedures for making copies?

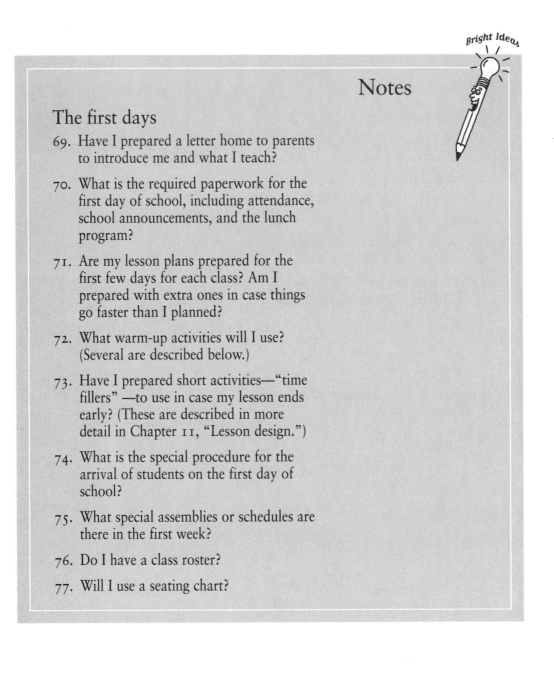

Bright Ideas

Notes

The first days

69. Have I prepared a letter home to parents to introduce me and what I teach?

70. What is the required paperwork for the first day of school, including attendance, school announcements, and the lunch program?

71. Are my lesson plans prepared for the first few days for each class? Am I prepared with extra ones in case things go faster than I planned?

72. What warm-up activities will I use? (Several are described below.)

73. Have I prepared short activities—"time fillers"—to use in case my lesson ends early? (These are described in more detail in Chapter 11, "Lesson design.")

74. What is the special procedure for the arrival of students on the first day of school?

75. What special assemblies or schedules are there in the first week?

76. Do I have a class roster?

77. Will I use a seating chart?

Feeling overwhelmed?

Many teachers feel overwhelmed with all they have to do to get ready. The checklist is designed to help alleviate some of those feelings, by grounding the anxiety into specific things that teachers can do.

You probably won't be able to address everything before the first day of school. Just address what you think is most important first, and leave the rest for various times throughout the first quarter. As a matter of fact, much of the information will come to you naturally, even if you don't go looking for it. Things like class rosters or special schedules will be provided for you, even if you don't ask for them.

Another way to make the days before school a little less anxious is to divide your to-do list (a combination of what's on the Before-School-Checklist and what's floating around in your head constantly) into two categories:

Mrs. Allgood says

Much of the information will come to you naturally, even if you don't go looking for it.

- ▲ Things to do before school starts
- ▲ Things to do in the first two weeks of school

Some of the items on your list will overlap both categories. For example, if you want to include your students in designing rules and consequences, you can determine the lesson plan strategy for this before school starts, and actually implement it in the first few days of school. Or, you can determine most of your classroom procedures before the students arrive, and implement/teach them in the first few weeks once school starts. By dividing your tasks into two categories, you can reduce your anxiety by reducing the things you need to do right away.

A Closer Look

You can determine most of your classroom procedures before the students arrive, and implement/teach them in the first few weeks once school starts.

Ask a veteran

You can get help completing the Before-School-Checklist by asking a veteran teacher at your new school. She not only knows the ropes, but also can offer perspective on the school's culture and political climate.

How to make use of extra time

It may seem crazy to add things to the list, but with efficient planning, extra time may be available. Try previewing novels, textbooks, videos, and/or computer software slated for student use. Create assignments and tests, purchase special supplies, decorate the classroom—even update your teacher wardrobe. Don't forget to leave messages for friends that you'll be busy and unavailable until June!

What if you're hired at the last minute?

I got my first job on Thursday afternoon, September 30th, a month after school had started. That night I attended Back-to-School Night and introduced myself to the parents of the students I hadn't yet met. A year prior to that, I was given a two-month long-term substitute job at 8:15 AM on a Monday, and my first class had started fifteen minutes earlier. First, I was handed a set of novels I'd neither heard of nor taught; then I was introduced to the class and set loose. Unfortunately, these scenarios are all too common.

Mrs. Allgood says

> Don't forget to leave messages for friends that you'll be busy and unavailable until June!

Though being tossed directly into the fire is not an ideal way to start, there are strategies that make it easier. Since developing lesson plans is the top priority, avoid assigning mountains of homework that will necessitate heavy grading time in the first week or two. This tack also will free up some time for the Before-School-Checklist. In this "emergency" situation, the two most critical questions on the checklist are: "Do I have a buddy and/or mentor teacher?" and "Do I have phone numbers of colleagues I can ask for help?" Refer to the section in this chapter called "what to do first?" on page 131.

This is barreling down the interstate, holding the wheel with one hand and the driver's instruction manual with the other. The good news is that there are always teachers out there who are willing to help, and that the learning is incredibly fast. Questions that cause a swerve on the first day will be easily addressed two weeks later. It's akin to how some young children learn a second language. There is a silent period where they absorb information without speaking, then all of sudden, bam!—full sentences.

Room arrangement

When setting up a classroom, there's a lot to consider:

Mrs. Allgood says

When newly hired and dropped into the class, avoid assigning mountains of homework that will necessitate heavy grading time in the first week or two.

▲ Does the arrangement maximize the physical safety of the students? Are heavy or sharp items secure? Is there ample room for students to move without elbowing each other?

▲ How close are the students to the front of the room? Closer is better for learning content and behavior.

▲ How close are students to each other? Close enough to share with a partner, far enough apart not to distract.

▲ How easy is it for the teacher to circulate among all her students?

▲ How easy is it for students to walk to and from the water fountain, pencil sharpener, and front door?

▲ Can students see the teacher, the TV, and the board?

▲ Are all students able to face forward during whole class instruction?

▲ Are frequently used materials stored with easy access? Are they so nearby that they cause a distraction?

- ▲ Are there personal touches in the room, such as plants, pets, or photos?
- ▲ Are the walls and bulletin boards decorated with posters, quotations, themes, student work? It helps to keep things simple at the start, adding student work as it is generated.
- ▲ Are computers placed towards the perimeter of the class to create a calm work environment for users?
- ▲ Are there places for students to put their coats and lunches (primarily elementary school)?
- ▲ Are there areas for student centers (also primarily for elementary school)? These won't need to be accessed in the first few days.

Seating arrangements should match the activities that you are doing. For direct instruction, there is nothing wrong with rows, even for younger students. For cooperative learning, group work, classroom community meetings, small group activities and the like, the seats need to be arranged differently. The seating formation can be changed frequently, as long as the students are taught and retaught the procedures for moving desks. In his book, *Tools for Teaching*, classroom management consultant Fred Jones maps out and critiques a variety of useful seating arrangements.

Mrs. Allgood says

> The seating formation can be changed frequently, as long as the students are taught and retaught the procedures for moving desks.

One design strategy is to use a large sheet of chart paper and post-it-notes. The chart paper represents the size of the room, and the post-it-notes represent each student desk and the personal space around it. Use a tape measure in your classroom to get a precise ratio. Rearrange the post-it-note "desks" on the chart paper, and use markers to indicate computers, tables and other items. Then go into your classroom and do the real thing.

Starting School

Activities for the first few days

Students want to be able to relax in our classroom. To do this, they want to know certain logistical things the minute they walk in the room for the first time, and certain more qualitative things in the first few days:

A Closer Look

To be able to relax in the classroom, students need to feel both physically and emotionally safe.

- ▲ Am I in the right room?
- ▲ Where should I sit?
- ▲ What do I need to do in order to succeed?
- ▲ Who is the teacher?
- ▲ Does the teacher care about me?
- ▲ Who are the other students in the room?
- ▲ Is this classroom safe, both physically and emotionally?
- ▲ What kind of classroom community will this be?
- ▲ What are the rules of this class?
- ▲ What will be expected of me?

Addressing these potential concerns early on maximizes the level of engagement they will have in their new environment. There are many activities we can do in the first few days that will help provide answers to these questions. Some teachers prefer to do very structured teacher-oriented activities the first few days of school, to establish the class routines and expectations. Others prefer to start with energizers and community building activities. There is no best way. However, if you are going to use energizers, make sure to teach the procedures clearly beforehand. And if you are going to use teacher-oriented activities, make sure to make strong connections with your students from the outset.

People Hunt

This is like a treasure hunt, where students seek information about each other. Each student has a sheet of criteria, such as "Find two people in the room who speak more than one language" or "who had a birthday this summer." The People Hunt can be done "tea-party style" where students are free to mingle and meet each other. It can also be done in a more structured way, where there are two circles, inner and outer, with students in the inner circle facing outward to face a partner in the outer circle. Each pair gets a certain amount of time, perhaps a minute or so per person, to ask four questions of each other from their People Hunt list. The teacher then rings a chime and the inner circle rotates counterclockwise, so that new partnerships are formed. This more structured activity ensures that everyone is included, and exclusive cliques don't get a chance to form.

Interviews

Students pair off and interview each other, then introduce their partners to the class. Please note that this activity might occupy two class periods for a secondary class of thirty students, but is usually shorter with younger kids. Variation: Students pair off and choose letter A or B. The B's speak for one minute, initiating with "I don't know" statements such as, "I don't know where you live," "I don't know your favorite color," "I don't know what sports you like," "I don't know what you did this summer," "I don't know what your favorite music is," or "I don't know how you feel about being back at school." Then the A's speak for two minutes responding to the B's statements, and filling in whatever blanks they want to in the B's knowledge. The level of risk is lower, because the A's can speak to topics with which they feel most comfortable. The process is then reversed so that both people get "interviewed." Then students can introduce each other or simply say one thing about their partner to the whole class.

The big lie

"How did you spend your summer vacation?" The twist to this one is that students have to make up the biggest lie they can. This frees up their imagination immensely, and offers a window into their personalities when they present to the class.

Variation: Two truths and a lie. Students write or speak about their summer vacation, including three key things they did. Two of them are true and one false. The process of the other students' guessing which is the lie can become a contest.

Goals and expectations / rules and consequences

The teacher goes over her goals for the year, and her expectations of her students — both academic and behavioral. Remember that this information should be taught in the same way that we teach content, by breaking items down into parts and checking for understanding. One idea is to require a score of 100% on a quiz of class principles, rules, and consequences. Students can take the quiz as often as necessary. Please refer to Chapter 12, "Rules and Consequences," for more on this strategy, along with "Student Participation in Rules and/or Consequences."

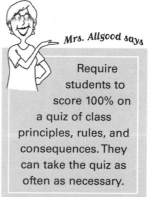

Mrs. Allgood says

Require students to score 100% on a quiz of class principles, rules, and consequences. They can take the quiz as often as necessary.

Self-evaluation from the future

Students can evaluate their upcoming school year as if it just ended, either filling out an evaluation form or writing a more free-flowing self-evaluation letter. This is a creative way that students can set goals and look at the long term. At the end of the school year, have them evaluate themselves again, and then give back their September evaluations for comparison. Some teachers of high school freshmen do a written goal-setting activity, and then return the papers to their students four years later at graduation.

Action thermometer

Initially, this can work similarly to the People Hunt, but with a twist. Students move to different sides of the room (or stand in place) if they have **done** a particular thing, **know** a particular thing, or **like** a particular thing. This can be used throughout the school year, with a focus on getting the students to know each other, or with a focus on forming small groups in the classroom. For example, "Please go to this side of the room if you like dogs better than cats, and that side of the room if you like cats better than dogs." Or "Stand up if you flew on a plane this summer." Or "Go to that side of the room if you speak at least two languages." In Chapter 11, "Lesson Design," using the action thermometer for teaching content is explained in detail.

Non-competitive musical chairs

Mrs. Allgood says

One good rule is: "If any student hits the floor, the game is over."

Chairs are arranged in a circle, facing in. The one chairless person stands in the middle, picks a criterion — such as, "If you are wearing green, get up and change seats" — and then he scrambles for a seat with the others. The one person who can't find a seat then stands in the center and the procedure is repeated with a different criterion. Criteria can be drawn from what students are wearing, where they've lived or traveled, languages they speak, or movies they've seen. Later on in the year, criteria can shift to class content. For example, each student is assigned a letter of the alphabet. A word is announced, and only those students whose letter appears in the word have to get up and switch chairs. Please note: this can get quite competitive. One good rule is: "If any student hits the floor, the game is over."

Name contest

Students compete to see who can say everyone's name in the class. Winners, and there can be more than one, receive a prize. If many of the students know each other from the previous year, but new students have also joined the school, the new students can try to name half of the students.

Whether or not students' names become the subject of a game, it helps when students learn each other's names early in the school year in order to begin to build a sense of community. One simple way is to provide students with name tags. Another is to give them an extra-credit, written quiz on one another's names.

Wise Apple Advice

A last thought about being prepared

I've already dragged one secret from my closet: as a new teacher, most of my lesson planning was done the night before I taught. It wasn't until January that it even occurred to me that it was *possible* to plan whole units in advance of teaching them. Once I figured that out, my stress level dropped and I was a more resilient teacher.

For most new teachers, preparing well in advance is a mythical goal, but every ounce of effort nets a triple return. In order to maximize preparation, take a look at the big picture. What **units** are scheduled? What **preparation** is necessary for each unit? What can be done **in advance**? What are the expected **outcomes** for each unit? In addition to the information above, check for several suggestions in Chapter 11, "Lesson Design."

▲ ▲ ▲

What to Do First?

There are four areas of focus that can help you get ready and reduce your anxiety:

- ▲ Before the first day
- ▲ Procedures
- ▲ Behavior
- ▲ Content

Before the first day

Refer to the Before-School-Checklist on page 116. If you have several weeks before school starts, read through the checklist and address as many questions as you can. If time is short and you have only a few days before the kids arrive, read through the whole list and mark those items which you think are most important. Start with those. Generally speaking, first put your focus on the basics:

▲ Teachers you can ask for help (discussed in Chapter 4, "Ask for Help")
▲ Room Arrangement (discussed on page 125)
▲ Bell schedule
▲ Classroom supplies for the first days
▲ Seating chart

Procedures

A list of procedures appears on page 83. Which ones do you do first? There are some standard procedures which you'll need to address almost immediately:

▲ Special assemblies or schedules on the first day
▲ When students first enter the classroom. How will you greet the students? How will they know where to sit?
▲ Quiet signal (page 93)
▲ Hand-raising for discussions
▲ Starting the class or lesson (sponge/warm-up activities, page 138)
▲ Distributing and collecting materials
▲ Bathroom policy
▲ Dismissing the class at the end of the class, the lesson, or the day

In addition to these, there are other procedures more tailored to your specific class. Decide what content you want to cover in the first week. Then determine which procedures the students will need to know in order to be able to cover that content. Remember to take time to teach the procedures. Have the students practice them until they know them well; then review them periodically throughout the first few weeks.

Take extra time in the first few weeks to lay down the railroad tracks of procedures. It's worth it!

Behavior

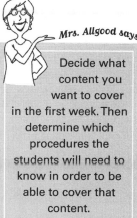

Mrs. Allgood says

Decide what content you want to cover in the first week. Then determine which procedures the students will need to know in order to be able to cover that content.

- ▲ Be ready with a list of rules (page 165) and consequences (page 175) or a plan for getting students involved in designing the rules and consequences (page 180)
- ▲ Prepare a quiz on the rules (page 182)
- ▲ Talk to the students about the importance of rules. Model appropriate behavior in specific situations.

Content

Be ready with lesson plans for the first week. It helps to make your first lessons more teacher-directed. Fill up the time with structured learning activities. As the kids get used to following your directions and getting to work, they perceive you as reliably in control. This helps create a feeling of safety and focus in the classroom.

There is nothing wrong with including ice-breakers and getting-to-know-you lessons (see page 127) in the first week, as long as the activities are structured and the procedures are taught and retaught.

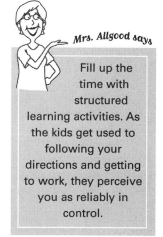

Mrs. Allgood says

Fill up the time with structured learning activities. As the kids get used to following your directions and getting to work, they perceive you as reliably in control.

Gather extra lesson ideas to fill the time (see "filler" on page 152) in case you are done early.

Design strategies for teaching the procedures that guide your lessons. Content can tend to go more slowly than new teachers think because of the time needed to teach these procedures. But it can also tend to go quickly because of teacher nervousness — rushing through ideas without including wait time or a full checking for understanding.

11

LESSON DESIGN

"Student divided by confusion equals algebra."

— LAURIE HALSE ANDERSON

CLASSROOM MANAGEMENT doesn't occur in a vacuum. It is intricately tied to what we teach and how we teach it. Lessons that motivate and engage kids keep management problems at a minimum. Mrs. Allgood always appears to do this well, providing her students with creative and meaningful activities. When things hit a lull, she simply comes up with a new idea that "wows" the kids, nipping their boredom in the bud.

How do we emulate Mrs. Allgood to make our lessons motivate as well as inform? How do we address the nitty-gritty — the daily requirements of organization — while still packing zip into our teaching? Let's look at some possible approaches. This chapter is organized like an effective lesson plan, starting first with a look at an overview of the big picture – the five step lesson plan - moving into increasingly greater detail, and closing with a close look at closure.

The Big Picture

Let's start with an overview of the five-step lesson plan which can be a valuable template in organizing, executing, and reflecting on your lessons:

Bright Ideas

The five-step lesson plan

Introduction

▲ Refer to previous lessons/units
▲ Point to what's coming
▲ Whet the students' appetites
▲ Assess students abilities / past performance

Direct instruction

▲ Direct the learning
▲ Facilitate, without necessarily lecturing
▲ Assess students

Guided practice

▲ Provide opportunities for students to work with new material/ideas
▲ Guide students through the process
▲ Assess students

Independent practice

▲ Encourage student autonomy
▲ Recognize the benefits to long-term memory development
▲ Choose appropriate homework, a prime example of independent practice
▲ Assess students

Closure

▲ Review what has happened
▲ Emphasize key points
▲ Point to what will happen next
▲ Assess students

Unpacking the lesson

The traditional five-step lesson plan, though by no means a requirement, can be an easy way to organize lessons. If students are acting out, try rearranging elements or reallocating the amount of time for each one.

▲ If students can't focus during independent practice, it may be because they need more direct instruction or more guided practice.

▲ If students receive new learning in the form of work-sheets, reluctant learners may have a hard time processing the material. If they have not first been taught that which they are supposed to practice, they may begin to act out.

▲ If too much time is spent on direct instruction without giving students a chance to work with the new material, they may get frustrated and/or bored, and begin to act out.

▲ If the closure step is skipped, students will tend to remember less, and then come back the next day feeling inadequate or antsy.

A Closer Look

Mrs. Meanswell starts designing her lesson by focusing on what she will *teach*. Mrs. Allgood starts by focusing on what she wants the students to *learn*.

Try using the five-step lesson plan as a template **before** teaching a particular unit. **Afterward**, if kids acted out, compare what actually happened in class with the template. Often, improved organization will decrease misbehavior.

A note on assessment. Assessment guides design. It can be formal, in the form of quizzes, tests, portfolio review, and grades. It can be informal, based on a show of hands, feedback, questionnaires, or teacher's sixth sense. It can also be a product of students assessing themselves or each other. Effective teaching involves a constant assessment "feedback loop" between teacher and students, and a responsiveness of the teacher to what the students need.

Designing lessons

Mrs. Meanswell starts designing her lesson by focusing on what she will teach. Mrs. Allgood starts by focusing on what she wants the students to learn. The steps of any good lesson trace a natural progression, connecting students' prior knowledge with what the teacher wants them to walk away with. Just connect the dots: "You are here; We're going *there*." This helps us focus on student learning, even as we hone in on the logistics of the lesson.

Starting the Lesson

How a lesson starts goes a long way in determining how smoothly the class runs and how much the kids learn. The first step sets the tone and direction.

Strategies

Silent work to begin a lesson or transition

Mrs. Allgood says

> Assign several sponge activities, so that overachievers have something to do while underachievers are still focused on the first item. Design at least one open-ended question each time.

There are dozens of strategies for silent work, often referred to as "sponges." Beginning a lesson in silence gives students a chance to focus, relax, and open the file cabinet in their brains to the topic at hand. And it gives us a chance to dispense with any individual student issues, without having to worry about the "Popcorn Effect," that troublesome tendency of the group to lose focus when we have private conversations in the classroom (for more on this, see Chapter 9, "Consistency"). These "sponge" activities can be anything we normally have students do, as long as they can do it silently and without having to ask for directions or clarifications.

Ideally, we want to design these activities so no one will finish before it's time for the next step. One method is to assign several activities, so that overachievers have something to do while underachievers are still focused on the first item. When everyone is done with the first item, call the class to order. Extra work done by overachievers can be addressed in class or collected for extra credit.

Another method is to design at least one open-ended question for each warm-up. For example, ask students to come up with as many words as they can using two or more letters from the word "cornucopia" or the word "abundance." (More about early finishers is addressed toward the end of this chapter.)

Refer to the previous lesson

Ask students to describe what the class did the day before. Ask key memory and analysis questions about the previous lesson. Look at the big picture of the unit and note how yesterday's lesson fit into the big picture. Giving students a look at where they've been, where they are, and where they are going can help them anchor what they are learning into long-term memory.

Give an overview of the lesson

Post an agenda for the lesson. Describe what's coming and why. Place the day's lesson in the context of the big picture of the unit, and perhaps the big picture of the whole year. Focus as much as possible on the goal — what students should learn during the lesson — rather than on what they will be doing.

> *A Closer Look*
>
> Anticipate and address potential student concerns up front. "Sell" the lesson.

Connect the lesson to the students' lives and the real world

If Sally understands the connection between what she's about to study and the potential of succeeding in volleyball or at her job or in getting along with her best friend, she's much more likely to focus. If that link isn't happening, try to get her "into" the lesson. For example, she can relate to the experiences of a character in the book she's reading in English class. She can imagine living in the time period she is studying in Social Studies.

The frame

How we frame a lesson has a huge effect on its success. Relating it to the students, as described above, is one way. Another is to embrace the worst by anticipating students' potential, legitimate concerns and addressing them up front. This idea is more immediately obvious to middle school and high school teachers who teach the same lesson more than once a day. As the day progresses, clues emerge that can help frame our lesson so students will be more interested. Two examples follow.

One day I showed the first part of the movie *Casablanca* to my high school students. I assumed that they would love the movie, since it is clearly one of the best ever made (no bias here at all…), but my first period students hated it! They complained, "It's boring! It's slow!" So, for second period, I introduced the movie by asking the students what a classic movie was. We discussed and brainstormed the differences between a classic movie and MTV, such as black-and-white versus color, and few camera angles versus many. Then I asked the students to take a deep breath and focus on s-l-o-w-i-n-g d-o-w-n in order to appreciate the subtleties of a truly classic movie. They ended up not only loving it, but also requesting the second part the next day. In contrast, without my successful framing, first-period students complained that they had to watch more of "that dumb movie."

> The three themes of my technology unit were "Chaos, Frustration, and Fun."

Several years ago, I taught a technology project, where students made personal and historical timelines using HyperStudio. Any time students use technology, I anticipate problems, and my students experienced every single possible snafu. There weren't enough computers, some computers froze, and data was lost. Despite the problems, they created spectacular finished projects, but I was one burned-out teacher, having had to fight my students the whole way.

Fool that I was, the next year I decided to do it again. But this time I introduced the unit differently. I wrote the word "chaos" in the upper left corner of the board, and told the students that it would be one of the themes of the unit. I laid out for them all of the things that could go wrong. Then I listed a second theme under "chaos" – "frustration" — an inevitable reaction to the chaos that results when technology breaks down. Finally, I added the word "fun," and said that if the students didn't fight the chaos and the frustration — if they didn't give up when things went wrong, but instead took them in stride — they would arrive at the third theme of the unit.

Sure enough, during the project, things went wrong. But this time, the students were much more tolerant. Somewhere in the middle of the unit, I asked students for a show of hands. "How many are in chaos?" One third of the hands went up. "How many are in frustration?" Another third. "How many are having fun?" One more third of the hands went up. "Everyone please look at those who are having fun," I said, "and know that this is your future, if you don't get too sidetracked by the chaos and the frustration." At the end of the unit, the projects were again spectacular, but this time I needed no stitches.

Remember, the frame sells the content of the lesson. Make it compelling, make it meaningful, make it novel, make it sexy.

Check for understanding of the day's procedures before and during each lesson

Mrs. Meanswell just hates this scenario: she's described everything that's going to take place, then asked for questions — and no one peeped. "Great," she thinks. "They've got it." She then releases the students to get started, and is immediately inundated with a sea of students asking what to do — or she looks out across a sea of students spacing out, avoiding her gaze but doing nothing because they have no idea what to do next.

Many times students will ask no questions, and yet many won't know what was just said. Mrs. Meanswell can alleviate part of the problem by changing the way she checks for understanding. It's usually not enough to tell the class what's coming next and then simply ask if students have questions.

One thing she can do is to ask individual students to repeat what the upcoming procedure is. Another is to ask them to pair off and have each person describe it to his partner as if the partner had just walked in the room. A third is to have students repeat it to their partners as if their partners were much younger than they, at an age she designates. A fourth is to ask questions that are targeted to specific parts of the overall procedure. She also could try the standard practice of writing procedures on the board, the overhead, a flip chart, and/or a handout.

Here's an example of one effective way to check for understanding:

"In a moment, José, I'm going to ask you to please repeat back to the class exactly what is going to happen next. Before you do, I'm going to ask two people to serve as monitors, to make sure that what you say is complete and accurate. Let's see… Sally, will you serve as a monitor? Great. And the other monitor? I'll decide after José has finished talking. So listen closely to what he says."

Assuming that Sally hasn't been paying attention, and assuming José is an overachiever and certainly has been paying attention, this example serves several purposes.

First, Sally isn't embarrassed for not knowing the procedure. She gets to learn it from José. Not only does she avoid embarrassment, she's empowered, because she now is seen as the authority or judge of José's response. She knows José is an overachiever and will know the answer, so she can feel secure in scoring his answer with high marks.

Second, the class gets to listen to the directions repeated by someone other than the teacher, the novelty of which will tend to increase their attention.

Third, José gets empowered because he was paying attention and was able to repeat back the correct procedure.

Fourth, everyone will tend to listen closely because they don't know who will be called on at the end to be the second monitor. The teacher can raise the stakes a bit by letting the class know she'll ask a follow-up question of the second monitor that goes beyond Sally's responsibility.

This process avoids singling Sally out with, "Sally, what did I just say?" — and then the inevitable, "Why weren't you paying attention?" Instead, Sally becomes an expert, and everybody benefits.

Some kids will be absent

We must plan for this! Otherwise we'll have a sea of questions and complaints at the start of the day or class: "What did I miss?" "Did we do anything important yesterday?" "What should I do today?" "I don't have the homework because I wasn't here yesterday" "Did you do anything while I was gone?"

Ask administrators and other teachers how they address the issue of absent students. Some schools have standard procedures for parents to pick up homework for their children. In addition, some suggestions are:

- ▲ Find a place in the room for extra handouts
- ▲ Use board space or butcher paper to display lessons/homework for each week
- ▲ Have a para-educator (instructional aide) prepare packets for absent students
- ▲ Use a student log-book (described below)
- ▲ Use a student buddy system, where students are responsible for contacting each other at home
- ▲ Coordinate with the office for communicating assignments to parents

Student logbook

Students keep track of daily activities and assignments. I tried this with a lot of success, and it was effortless for me. Each day a different student was assigned to take careful notes on what we did in class and details of the homework assignment. The next

I love it when kids come back after an absence and say "Did you do anything while I was gone?"

day when an absent student returned, he would look in the log-book to catch up. If, after looking in the logbook, he had to ask me what he missed, then the student who wrote the log would not receive credit for doing it.

One variation I developed turned out to be even simpler. I'd allow certain students do the log for extra credit. This helped ensure that good note-takers were the ones who did the work.

> If, after looking in the logbook, he had to ask me what he missed, then the student who wrote the log would not receive credit for doing it.

There are two side benefits of the logbook. First, at the end of the year I had documentation of every-thing that had transpired, which I used as an auxil-iary lesson plan book for the next year. Second, early in the term, the book's cover became the subject of a class art contest. Since each of the four sides of the notebook were covered, four students could win. Thus, the log-book was beautiful, and students took pride in it.

Accepting late work

How many days late should we accept student work? Much of the decision depends on the culture of the school. One teacher I know didn't accept work that was more than one week late. Her bulletin board was divided into five sections labeled Monday through Friday, and each day's homework list was posted there. One week after its original due date, the teacher removed each list. For example, on Wednesday the eleventh, she removed the homework assignment that had been due on Wednesday the fourth, and replaced it with the current homework assignment.

Like most teachers, she provided a standard deduction in points for late work. How much to deduct is a an individual deci-sion, but please remember that kids often have legitimate reasons for being late. Further, if students are chronically late with quali-ty work, a rigid late policy may discourage them from ongoing effort and participation. We need to design clear systems, but allow room for forgiveness.

Delay classwork that's based on homework

It helps to delay class work one or two days when it is based on homework so that late homework assignments can be addressed in class.

As a new teacher, I often had students respond to and edit each other's writing in groups. One day, twelve of my twenty-seven students came to school unprepared. They hadn't written their rough drafts, and thus couldn't really do the activity I had planned. So I gave them a chance to write quietly while the other fifteen students worked in small response groups. This was a mistake, because:

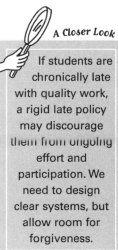

A Closer Look

If students are chronically late with quality work, a rigid late policy may discourage them from ongoing effort and participation. We need to design clear systems, but allow room for forgiveness.

▲ Students who didn't do their homework were rewarded with class time in which to do it
▲ They were deprived of valuable group response time
▲ My attention during the class was divided by having to keep the writers quiet when I really ought to have been fully focused on the response groups
▲ The overall quality of student work suffered

I then realized I should collect rough drafts on Tuesday, and hand them back on Thursday for the student response groups. This gave late students an extra two days to complete the homework assignment — outside of class. While I held them accountable for being late, they had a buffer zone before the response groups took over. For Tuesday and Wednesday I planned other, related activities.

I then realized I should collect rough drafts on Tuesday, and hand them back on Thursday for the student response groups.

▲ ▲ ▲

The Lesson Itself

When a lesson works, not only do students learn and retain information, they also tend to behave well, because they're engaged in the learning. To help make a lesson work, there are many things one can do.

Strategies

Variety

I remember teaching an incredibly powerful lesson to my ninth-grade class-from-heck. They were in a circle taking turns completing sentences such as, "I am proud that…," or "I really care about…" Light bulbs were going off in their heads. They were hungry to express and hungry to appreciate each other's expressions. But after about fifteen minutes, the hunger started to erode. Kids started making side comments and fidgeting in their seats. My comments, formerly on the order of, "Thank you for sharing and listening," began to be replaced by, "Shh!" and "Please stay focused." As fulfilling as the exercise was, they needed variety.

Mrs. Allgood says

> Try planning at least three activities per lesson — at least one of which has you off-stage — and switch activities at least three times every fifty minutes.

We should plan at least three activities per lesson — at least one of which has the teacher off-stage — and switch activities at least three times every fifty minutes. In addition, employ shifts in focus and energy at least every ten to twelve minutes (see "movement breaks" on page 155). For example, if we have students doing oral reports, every ten minutes they can write a summary or highlight or talk to a neighbor about their highlights. But regardless, try not to spend the whole period on oral reports. Build in other things to do as well, such as an opening warm-up activity, and a closing brain-teaser.

Legal talking

When possible, make talking 'legal' in the classroom. If students are supposed to be doing a worksheet at their desks silently and there are islands of conversation or laughter or clucking sounds, then all the students perceive that the teacher is not doing her job to address the noise. So she has to constantly put out sparks before they combust into fires. This makes her a fire fighter. And it means that most of her energy is focused on making the room quiet, rather than on addressing student questions about the worksheet.

The brain loves to talk. Providing students opportunities to work together can remove the necessity for absolute quiet while increasing attention, energy, and retention. One solution is to pair off students and have them do the worksheet together. Then, talking is "legal," and some noise in the room is expected. The teacher is free to put her energy where it belongs — focused on content.

In structuring this kind of activity, either the teacher or the students can designate partners, and final papers can be individual or pair submissions. One of my favorite scenarios is to have each student hand in his own paper, stapled to his partner's. I then grade them separately, and choose either the lower grade or one randomly selected as the grade for both partners. While this doesn't guarantee that the pair truly worked together in a democratic fashion, it does ensure that at least both students have written down the same answers.

One more variation is to make the worksheets into a game. Call it a treasure hunt. Give the teams ten minutes to "find" as many answers as possible. Collect the sheets at the end, and return them the next day with prizes for the winners — in the form of recognition, points, sports cars... This competition will ensure that no pairs of people talk with any other pairs, and students will tend to focus the entire time.

Mrs. Allgood says

Pair off students and have them do the worksheet together. Then, talking is "legal," and some noise in the room is expected. We are free to put our energy where it belongs — focused on content.

Assume the best when students don't answer

Silence in response to a question does not necessarily mean that students don't know the answer, nor does it mean that they are being belligerent. They could:

- ▲ Be intimidated
- ▲ Be able to answer part, but not all of the question
- ▲ Need more time to process the question or
- ▲ Need the question or lesson broken into smaller parts

One strategy successful with younger students is to give each of them three index cards with traffic signals drawn on each. One depicts a red light, one a yellow light, and one a green light. To check for understanding in a lesson, simply ask students to hold up one of their cards. Green means they understand the lesson and are ready for more. Yellow means they could use a few examples or illustrations. Red means they have no idea what's going on. A quick scan of the room will provide a cue as to what to do next.

Students can also hold a thumb up, sideways, or down to indicate quality of understanding of the lesson.

Slow down delivery

Our second language learners and/or special needs students often require more time to process information. One way we can help accommodate their needs is by speaking more slowly and repeating ourselves more. This simple act can make a world of difference for some of our students.

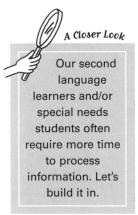

A Closer Look

Our second language learners and/or special needs students often require more time to process information. Let's build it in.

Increase wait time

As a new teacher, I remember being so nervous that I would never allow time for students to process my questions. Silence meant that somehow I was doing something wrong or the students were off-task. In reality, students often need more time to think than we think. Try silently timing the gaps between when you ask a question and when it appears no one has an answer. Sometimes we need to wait ten or fifteen seconds before students begin to raise their hands with responses — it can seem like an eternity.

Wait for several hands to be raised

Teachers often call on the first student to raise his hand. This ultimately can mean that the teacher and one or two students have a great lesson, but the rest of the students are left behind. One strategy is to tell the class that no one will be called on until at least eight hands are raised. It will take more time, but more students will use that time to process their answers and raise their hands.

Mrs. Allgood says

One strategy is to tell the class that no one will be called on until at least eight hands are raised.

Say "thank you," instead of "right"

When six students have their hands raised and the first one is called upon, don't acknowledge the correctness or incorrectness of his answer. Simply say, "Thank you," and call on the next student. After six or eight responses, provide the correct answer. This technique accomplishes several things. It increases the number of students who participate in a discussion, it encourages students to speak their ideas out loud because they aren't as intimidated about getting an answer wrong, and it focuses the students more on learning than on getting the answer right or impressing the teacher. It doesn't matter if five or ten students in a row say the same answer. Great. They are all actively participating.

Class choral recital

Every once in a while, ask all the students to say an answer out loud at the same time. It's novel, it gets their attention, and it increases their involvement. It's also safe for those who aren't sure of the answer, especially if they're reciting an answer after we've already given it to them.

Break things into parts — slow down content

Mrs. Allgood is quite a juggler. But she knows that if she hands each student three balls, and then performs a slick juggling demonstration, few students will catch on. However, it's a different story if she starts with one ball and then builds up from there, with regularly-scheduled stops to check for mastery and to offer hints. That way, just about all of her students can learn the basics of juggling in a relatively short period of time. Plus, their motivation will remain high, because they can mark and appreciate their progress as they learn.

Over the years she's learned to appreciate the important art of breaking learning into clear and doable steps — like adding stepping-stones across a stream. This is true not only with procedures and behavior, but with content as well. Mrs. Allgood seems to have handouts and manipulatives for every step of her lessons, allowing students to progress at whatever pace fits their abilities. Because she molds this strategy over her basic assumption that students want to learn, what seems like complex material is learned more easily in her classroom. This can be intellectually challenging. If Mrs. Meanswell, who is just learning how to do this, tried to break things into *too many* steps, she'd be hard pressed to do it.

A Closer Look

Like stepping stones in a stream, more steps equals faster learning.

Student success

As much as possible, build in success for students, even if the successes seem miniscule at first. Contrary to what some suggest, I believe we learn more from our successes than from our failures. When students experience success early and often, it helps build their confidence, which in turn helps them maintain their focus. It also helps their brains wire new information systematically. A series of positive, low-stress exposures to new knowledge is more likely to wire new learning into the brain than a series of negative, higher-stress experiences.

It is especially vital to make the initial steps in new learning small enough that students can master them. If the first step on the escalator is too high, they'll never get on it. As students gain confidence, we can make the steps more challenging. Ideally the steps should be small enough that students are able to take them, and large enough that students feel a sense of accomplishment as they go.

Grading vs. feedback

Mrs. Meanswell focuses on *grading* her students' work. Mrs. Allgood focuses on giving her students *feedback*. Grades are for parents and colleges. Feedback is for student learning. Once teachers understand that assessment is an aspect of teaching, they open up to a wide variety of ways to provide feedback to students in addition to grades — including oral critiques, comments by other students, publishing student work, portfolio review, providing rubrics, and reviewing assignments in class.

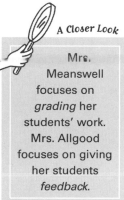

A Closer Look

Mrs. Meanswell focuses on *grading* her students' work. Mrs. Allgood focuses on giving her students *feedback*.

Clean slates

If students begin to feel overwhelmingly behind, create periodic "clean slates." A second chance can mean the difference between success and giving up from a lack of hope.

For example, when students have done poorly in the first quarter, try giving the second quarter's report card more weight than the first quarter's. Or, when quizzing students periodically to see if they are keeping up with the assigned reading in a novel, be inclusive. If there is a student who is always a day or two behind, he will fail every quiz. But if the quiz includes questions from chapters one through seven instead of only from chapter seven, for example, then the student will be more likely to feel successful, and to receive a passing grade.

When students finish early

Always anticipate what to do when some students are finished early with an in-class assignment. Put a permanent activity list on the wall, or write in advance on the board a specific, appropriate task. Ideally, these extra activities should be things early finishers can do in silence, without having to get out of their chairs; otherwise, prepare ahead of time for any potential disruption. For example, if the main activity is taking a test, followed by reading an awkward, crackly newspaper, students should *first* get newspapers, find the article to read, fold the paper, and place it on the floor next to their desk. *Then* they can take the test.

Create a generic list that can be used by early finishers — or for the entire class in case you are called on the phone, have a surprise visitor, or need to have an impromptu one-on-one talk with a student. Suggested activities include starting on homework, drawing a picture, making up a rhyming poem, doing a puzzle, solving riddles, answering extra credit questions, or reading in their novel, textbook, or the newspaper. Once kids are engaged and on-task, you can go about your business.

> *Mrs. Allgood says*
>
> Create a generic list of activities that can be used by early finishers — or for the entire class in case you are called on the phone, have a surprise visitor, or need to have an impromptu one-on-one talk with a student.

Filler

Filler is stuff we can plug into our lesson in a moment's notice if we need to fill up more time. Ideally, fill an emergency file with activities instantaneously available for that last five minutes, ten minutes, twenty minutes, or the whole lesson. When I first student-taught, this file was probably the most valuable thing I had.

Earlier in this chapter, in the paragraph on "variety," I referred to a risky creative lesson plan where each of my ninth-grade students took a turn finishing sentences like, "I am proud that...," or "I really care about..." Although engaged for the first fifteen minutes of this activity, noise slowly built up, followed by my voice as I tried to restore focus. Mercifully, the bell finally rang after the activity had continued about ten minutes longer than it should have.

My student-teaching supervisor was observing that day. After class she remarked that I should have ended the activity after fifteen minutes and moved on to something else. I told her I wholeheartedly agreed, that I had been aware of it at the time, but *I couldn't think of anything else the students could do*. Bottled up by my inexperience and my nervousness at creating a safe environment for my students to communicate personally to each other, I just painfully slogged through those last tough minutes. Today I can think of twenty or thirty things I could have used as filler. For example, I could have asked my students to move their desks back, take out a piece of paper and write reflectively about the activity for five minutes. Then they could have read their writing aloud to a partner or two. This could have been followed by a brief class discussion of what they wrote.

Where do we collect filler? Education catalogs sell "teacher survival guides," and effective teachers like Mrs. Allgood have many quality ideas they can share. Just keep your eyes peeled.

Teacher down-time

Mrs. Allgood says

Ideally, we should reserve five minutes at the start of each lesson and additional time in the middle where we are "off stage."

Ideally, teachers should reserve five minutes at the start of each lesson and additional time in the middle where they are "off stage," when they are not delivering content. While the class is writing, watching a video, working in small groups, or using computers, teachers can focus on individual issues or resolve problems. For example, if Mark disrupts a lesson because he wants to know why he can't turn in his homework late, simply redirect him to ask the same question during the group work that is coming up in four minutes. Talking to him privately during down-time avoids the dreaded "Popcorn Effect" discussed in Chapter 9, "Consistency."

For teachers of younger children, time off-stage can often seem like a myth. Nonetheless, there are times during the day that are better than others for addressing student issues. Identify these times in advance, cultivate them as much as possible in lesson plans, and take advantage of them every day.

If a lesson has the teacher "up front" all the time, students are likely to be exhausted at the end of the day. Their brains love to talk, move, and problem solve; when students are constantly sitting and listening to the teacher, they miss out on many active learning opportunities. Even more significantly, perhaps, is the benefit of teacher down-time for teachers: just knowing a respite is coming will provide invaluable peace of mind.

Frustration

Sometimes our students get frustrated. This is often a powerful and necessary ingredient for real learning — a process that often seems to be non-linear. We grow in leaps, sputters and spurts, which inevitably generates feelings of frustration. If our students push away the frustration, they don't stick around long enough to receive the wisdom that follows. Conversely, embracing frustration can often act like the irritation in the oyster than yields the pearl.

As teachers, we need to foster a positive attitude in our students toward feeling frustration in our classrooms. In his book *Emotional Intelligence*, Daniel Goleman points to various factors as indicators of emotional intelligence. One of them is the ability to delay gratification — which goes hand-in-hand with the ability to receive frustration without acting it out.

A Closer Look

Embracing frustration can often act like the irritation in the oyster than yields the pearl.

This concept is equally true for our own experiences. Teaching can be incredibly frustrating at times. If we welcome frustration as an essential part of learning, we will be less likely to take our stresses home with us, and more likely to grow and blossom as teachers. Plus, we will model this receptivity to our students, thus encouraging their learning and growth.

▲ ▲ ▲

Including all students

Countering bias

Teachers often feel most comfortable with people who seem the most familiar to them. While this in itself isn't problematic, it can lead to subtle, and not-so-subtle, biases in the classroom. As teachers we need to continually take stock to ensure that we treat all our students fairly, regardless of whether or not they differ from us or from other students. These differences can run along many lines, including personality type, physical and emotional challenges, gender, primary language, religion, and race. Though this book is not designed to explore this issue in detail, teachers need to address it so that bias in the classroom, ranging from subtle favoritism to outright racism, doesn't take place.

Wise Apple Advice

We need to continually take stock to ensure that we treat all our students fairly, regardless of whether or not they differ from us or from other students.

Multi-cultural education

We teach the whole person, and that includes student culture, background, nationality, and heritage. We can't ask students to leave their cultures outside the classroom door if we expect them to succeed. The more we can reach toward including the diverse cultures of our students, the more likely we will be able to reach them.

▲ ▲ ▲

Movement Breaks

Building in creative and enjoyable breaks can capture — or recapture — kids' attention, keep them actively involved, and break up the monotony of a lecture or discussion.

A Closer Look

We can't ask students to leave their cultures outside the classroom door if we expect them to succeed.

Breathing

Ask the students to take a deep breath, and then exhale together. They will enjoy watching the teacher model this almost as much as they'll enjoy doing it.

Stretching

This can be done in their seats with their arms over their heads, or standing up. Try breaking the lesson into "innings," and schedule in a 7th-inning stretch.

A Closer Look

Building in creative and enjoyable breaks can capture — or recapture — kids' attention, keep them actively involved, and break up the monotony of a lecture or discussion.

Cross-laterals

March in place and touch right hand to left knee and then left hand to right knee, or give yourself a pat on the back on the opposite side. This gets blood to the brain and activates both the right and left hemispheres.

Action thermometer

Place four phrases around the room: "Strongly Agree, Agree, Disagree, Strongly Disagree." Ask questions, and have students move to the phrase that represents their answer. Debate the issues, and as students change their opinions, they can move about the room.

Variation. Have students go to the right or left side of the room depending on their answers to a variety of questions. Examples: "If you are left-handed, have a pet at home, like Rock-and-Roll, prefer beaches to mountains." Or, make it content related: "If you think the answer is seventeen... if you think the character in the novel should say yes... if you think the main cause was economic..." Assign each student an element of the periodic table, and have them move to various places in the room depending on the number of electrons they have, or whether they are solid, liquid, or gas. Give younger children objects to hold, and have them sort by shape or texture or color. In history lessons, students can "become" historical figures, and sort around the room according to the field — politics, art, sports, music — in which they became famous.

Ball toss or frisbee throw

After a student catches the (soft) frisbee, he says one thing he's learned from the lesson. Then he tosses the frisbee to another student. This can be done with students in a circle, or while they are at their desks in their normal seating arrangement.

Closure

The last three minutes can be the most significant of any lesson, as they can markedly increase student retention. Rather than have kids put stuff in backpacks or cubbies, and mill about the room, actively engage them with closure activities. Mrs. Meanswell's closure often takes the form of looking at her watch and saying, "There's the bell. We'll continue this tomorrow. And don't forget your homework…"

Mrs. Allgood consistently focuses on closure. She doesn't frame her units as one big lesson that is haphazardly broken up by bells or other subject area studies. She deliberately designs beginnings and endings to each lesson that allow her students a chance to reflect on their learning, and that increase the likelihood that information will move from short-term to long-term memory.

Strategies

Reciprocal Teaching

Students pair off and take turns summarizing what the class did and/or learned, speaking as if their partners just showed up late for class.

Highlights

Students can come up with one or more key ideas from the lesson. They can write them down, speak them to a partner or the teacher, or simply take some silent reflection time. One way to frame the idea of highlights is to ask students what they could say that night at dinner when they are asked "What did you learn in school today?"

The big picture

For many students, learning in school is like walking through a cave with a small flashlight. They don't know what's up ahead, and they can't remember what they just passed. They focus entirely on where to put their next step, without remembering why they are in the cave in the first place. Make sure to refer to the bigger context of the lesson, or ask students to do it. What was done yesterday, what will be done tomorrow, and how will it all fit in with the unit and the school year?

Mrs. Allgood says

Students pair off and take turns summarizing what the class did and/or learned, speaking as if their partners just showed up late for class.

Provide a unifying metaphor

Sometimes a simple analogy or metaphor can "close the deal" on student learning by providing a "hook" that wires information into their brains. One example earlier in this chapter was the use of juggling to show the importance of breaking information into parts. An example from social studies class is comparing D-Day, the invasion of Normandy, to a surprise birthday party.

Homework

We've discussed creating a space on the board or wall where homework assignments are always posted. We can go one step further by clarifying that students are responsible for posted homework, *even if it isn't discussed in class.* This will create a safety net in case we get sidetracked.

Spend a minute or two before the class ends focusing on the specifics of the homework, how it relates to what was just studied. Check to see that all students have the assignment written down, and are clear about what they need to do that night to be successful.

Occasionally, this can include private discussions of what time they will do their homework, what room in their home, and what desk space. Many students don't have the support at home to do homework. By addressing this, we can help them find an appropriate environment, or perhaps facilitate their doing homework at school before they leave for the day.

Wise Apple Advice

The closure on closure

Whenever possible, have the students actively involved during closure. They can speak aloud to the class, to a partner, or a small group. Closure can also involve pictures and role playing, predictions about what's coming next, a look at the big picture, or a celebration of the day's learning. Even though closure takes away from time spent teaching new material, by slowing down we speed up. Extra time for making connections will increase retention and actually allow us to go faster in the long run.

INTERVENTION —
What We Do
In Response

Mrs. Meanswell:	I hope I didn't see you looking at Don's paper.
Mark:	I hope you didn't either.

12

RULES AND CONSEQUENCES

> *"We ask for strength and the Great Spirit gives us difficulties, which makes us strong."*
>
> — NATIVE AMERICAN PRAYER

ALL TEACHERS, either overtly or subtly, employ rules and consequences. This chapter is about how Mrs. Allgood uses them — both what she does and why she does it. It's divided into three main sections: principles, rules, and consequences. Principles are the underlying "big picture" goals for the class. Rules and consequences are specific classroom behavior policies that help support the principles.

Before getting into the details, let's take a look at the big picture. There is an ongoing philosophical debate in education about the need for and the use of consequences. This is discussed at the end of the chapter in the section called "Intrinsic vs. Extrinsic Motivation." My stance is that prevention should be the dominant focus of teachers, and that ideally, assuming the best about students, preparing, caring, and our inner authority are what make a true difference in the classroom and in our students' lives.

The reality is, however, that all of us, especially when we first start out, need stuff we can can use right away. And consequences are often the "stuff" that does the trick. Thus, this chapter has a lot of strategies and approaches in it. I don't try to sell any particular one. Try some of the strategies on and see if they fit. However, even as you use rules and consequences, please don't rely too heavily on them as a mechanical substitute for your genuine and personal enthusiasm for your students and their learning.

Principles

Principles are akin to guidelines. They are more general and often more value-laden than rules. They are not specific or behavioral in nature. But as opening "slogans" that are attached to rules, they can add a sense of underlying purpose and spirit to a list of rules and consequences. Many teachers include one or two principles as mission statements under which their rules appear. A few common principles are listed below.

A Closer Look

Principles can add a sense of underlying purpose and spirit to a list of rules and consequences.

- ▲ Treat each other fairly
- ▲ Respect and responsibility
- ▲ A safe place to learn
- ▲ Our classroom community
- ▲ The students have the right to learn and the teacher has the right to teach
- ▲ Safe, kind, and productive

Under any of these "umbrella" statements are five or six specific rules that "close the door" on potential misinterpretations from students.

Rules

Rules are what we can and can't live with in our classroom. They are what we would see in the classroom if our principles were being supported.

Strategies

Wording the rules

Rules should be specific, clearly stated, and worded behaviorally, rather than morally. If we leave the door open for misinterpretation of our rules, students will leap across the threshold. The more specific, behavioral, and clear our rules are, the skinnier students will have to be to fit through that doorway. For example, "Listen attentively while other students contribute to a class discussion," is a solid behavioral rule. Mrs. Meanswell often gets tripped up with student misinterpretation because her rules sound more like principles, such as "Respect each other."

Limit the number of rules to five or six at the most

We can't cover everything with only six rules, but we can address the big stuff. More than six rules will ultimately confuse and/or intimidate our students, while at the same time diluting the importance of the key rules that really matter to us.

The following are examples of specific classroom rules. Some are more appropriate for younger students, and some for older students. Some are very specific, covering only a very particular behavior, like gum chewing, while others are more fundamental.

> **Wise Apple Advice**
>
> Rules should be specific, clearly stated, and worded behaviorally, rather than morally.

- ▲ Follow directions
- ▲ Don't interrupt others' right to learn or my right to teach
- ▲ Be in your seat when the bell rings
- ▲ Follow all the school rules

▲ Listen attentively while other students contribute to a class discussion

▲ Keep hands, feet, and other objects to yourself

▲ Speak only at appropriate times

▲ Raise your hand and wait for permission to speak

▲ No put-downs

   ▲ Bring all books and materials to class

   ▲ No eating in class

   ▲ No gum-chewing in class

   ▲ Listen quietly when someone else is talking

   ▲ The teacher, not the bell, dismisses the class

   ▲ Use appropriate language

   ▲ Use a low-level voice in the classroom

   ▲ Touch other students' belongings only with their permission

▲ Place all trash in the basket

▲ You are responsible for completing your own work, unless group work is assigned

▲ There is no "arguing with the ref" during class. If you disagree with the teacher's decision, wait until after class to express your opinion (This is discussed in more detail in Chapter 9, "Consistency").

A Closer Look

There is no hard and fast rule about what rules should rule in the classroom — or what rules we should rule out.

Which rules to choose?

There is no hard and fast rule about what rules should rule in the classroom — or what rules we should rule out. It helps to avoid some typical miscues, as exemplified by Mrs. Meanswell's gaffes. She has rules that:

▲ She isn't organized enough to enforce—"Late work only accepted for three days, and for gradually reduced points"

▲ She doesn't feel strongly about, and thus doesn't enforce consistently — "No bathroom use during instructional time"

- ▲ Are too specific and don't cover enough territory — "Sharpen pencils quietly"
- ▲ She has copied from Mrs. Allgood across the hall, but isn't comfortable with —"No gum chewing"
- ▲ Aren't clear enough — "Respect each other"

In addition to avoiding the above mistakes, it is most important that our rules cover the main classroom behaviors and coordinate with school and district policies.

Consequences – Five Key Assumptions

Consequences are the bottom line, the cork in the bottom of the bucket that keeps the water from flowing out. Almost everything else in this book is about *prevention*. Consequences are about *intervention*. Even after we've done what we can in the areas of teaching procedures, assuming the best about our students, being firm and soft, not over-explaining, being consistent, and creating positive connections with our students, sometimes kids act out anyway. That's when consequences come in.

Below are five key assumptions about consequences, followed by a rather extreme example that illustrates all five.

- ▲ There are no punishments, just consequences
- ▲ Consequences are used as a pause to get our students' attention
- ▲ Consequences should be organized in a hierarchy, starting with the mildest first
- ▲ We have no control over our students
- ▲ Consequences teach students that they have the power of choice

A Closer Look

Consequences are the bottom line, the cork in the bottom of the bucket that keeps the water from flowing out.

Dan and the flying hammer

One day I was teaching woodshop as usual. I had already learned that classroom management in a woodshop class is absolutely critical, especially with my at-risk high school kids. I had to know the students could be trusted to take care of themselves and each other during those times when I was absorbed cutting wood and completely oblivious to their actions. Since natural consequences to "spacing out" in woodshop class can be permanent and disabling, such as the loss of a finger, my insistence on keeping kids focused in this class was even greater than in any other classes I taught.

On this day, I was using the table saw, which requires a high degree of concentration. Out of the corner of my eye I vaguely saw something coming toward me in the air — in surrealistic slow motion. A large "implement of destruction," a rotating hammer, slowly crossed my line of vision and careened onto the floor near my feet. I finished cutting my piece of wood, looked up in the direction from which the large implement of destruction had come, and immediately saw students scattering in the wind. Sara was suddenly fascinated with the wood planer. Eli had his nose in a book for the first time in his high school career. Dan, however, was caught like a deer in the headlights. It was clear from the position of his body and the guilty look on his face that I had found my source.

> A large "implement of destruction," a rotating hammer, slowly crossed my line of vision and careened onto the floor near my feet.

"Dan," I said in my firm-yet-soft teacher voice, "please come over here and let's talk a minute." All the machinery in the shop had stopped. All eyes were on Dan, waiting to see how this drama would play itself out.

He erupted immediately, coming toward me in a hail of defense: "I didn't! It wasn't me! You can't prove it! It wasn't a large hammer! It didn't go very far! No one was hurt! No!"

I remained as calm as I could, and simply said his name several times to calm him down. That didn't work. Whatever was going on with Dan went beyond this simple classroom experience. "Dan," I said again, firmly but quietly, "you need to go to the office, have a seat, and wait for me after class." This was a standard and mild consequence at my alternative school, used for a variety of behaviors much more benign than throwing hammers in the woodshop. Dan didn't leave, and he didn't stop his barrage of excuses and defenses. Twice more I asked him to leave, and finally I said, "Dan, if you don't choose to leave now, I'm going to have to suspend you for a day." This was a much more major consequence, one that I rarely had to use. But still Dan didn't leave nor quiet down. His arm movements and excuses kept coming in waves.

Finally I calmly said, "Dan, you're suspended." He stopped in his tracks. It was if his plane had suddenly landed, or his alarm clock had suddenly gone off.

"But," he began to implore.

"Please, Dan," I quietly responded, "don't make it any bigger than it has to be. Please go to the office and wait for me there." Dan finally decided to go. As soon as he left and the door closed, I looked up and suddenly the machinery was back on, Eli had abandoned his book, and class was back to its usual state of controlled chaos.

Dan was suspended that Tuesday afternoon, and he came back to school on Thursday morning with his father. Dan and his dad met the principal and me before school to work things out. Dan seemed his normal bumbling self, rather than his abnormal ranting self, and we had a relaxed conversation. Dan asked me why I suspended him, and I replied, "Dan, I didn't suspend you for throwing the hammer. I suspended you because it was the gentlest way I could find to get your attention. Do I have your attention now? Good. Let's talk about the rules of the woodshop…"

> My student had just thanked me for suspending him!

For five minutes, we had a cordial conversation. Dan convinced me that he could return safely to woodshop class, a class in which he actually excelled. We reviewed the rules, and that was that. As Dan was leaving the principal's office, he said to me, "Thank you, Mr. Smith," and walked out.

Something in that simple sentence set a light bulb off in my head. My student had just thanked me for suspending him! *He wanted to learn behavior*, he knew he needed to learn it, and he thanked me for suspending him. The consequence was there to provide him with the guidance that he was hungering for.

▲ ▲ ▲

The five key assumptions about consequences are all illustrated in the above story. First, **there are no punishments, just consequences.** I hadn't punished Dan; I had merely connected him with a simple consequence that did him the service of slowing him down. Even the extreme case of suspension is still a tool to teach students what they are hungry to learn.

Second, I realized that **consequences are used as a pause to get our students' attention.** It just so happened that in this case, suspension was what it took.

Third, I used **a hierarchy of consequences, starting with the mildest first.** I slowly and calmly increased the consequences for Dan, stopping with the first one that got him to pause in his tracks. For more on this approach, check the section below called "Implementing Consequences."

Fourth, during the confrontation with Dan, unless I used handcuffs, rope, or Velcro, **I had no control over him.** Calming down and ultimately following the rules were up to him. Yes, I had the power of suggestion. Yes, I could influence his decision with my voice, my tone, and/or the consequences I doled out, but ultimately the decision was his. The deeper our respect for this, the easier it is for us to remain calm and on our students' side in moments when we wish we had control over them.

A Closer Look

All choices bear fruit, whether sweet or bitter. It is our job to allow students to gently learn and internalize the sometimes wonderful and sometimes biting nature of responsibility.

Fifth, at the end of the meeting in the principal's office, it was affirmed that **Dan had the power of choice.** He became aware that he made a choice that day in the woodshop class to throw the hammer, a choice to argue with me, a choice to eventually leave the class and calm down, and a choice to abide by the rules in the future.

Let's look at this last assumption with a sharper lens. With choice comes responsibility. All choices bear fruit, whether sweet or bitter. It is our job to allow students to gently learn and internalize the sometimes wonderful and sometimes biting nature of responsibility. When we provide consequences for students, we are simply connecting them with the fruits of their choices, and giving them an opportunity to assess those choices.

For example, if Mark is talking to his neighbor while Mrs. Allgood is trying to explain something to the class, she can simply walk over to Mark's desk and stand next to him. In most cases, her proximity — the consequence — reminds him that he is talking out of turn. He reassesses his choices, asking himself:

"Am I talking out of turn? Yes.
Do I want to stop talking and pay attention? Yes, I think I do."

Mrs. Allgood's proximity is a consequence that gets Mark to pause and reassess the choice that he is making.

To take the scenario one step further — suppose Mark continues to talk when Mrs. Allgood moves away from his desk. She realizes that the consequence of proximity is too mild, so she chooses a different one. She says Mark's name. If that doesn't get him to pause and make a new choice, then she quietly informs him that if he continues to talk, he will have his seat changed. If that doesn't work, then she connects him with the next consequence in her hierarchy. This isn't done because Mark is bad or wrong, but because Mrs. Allgood is honoring her right to teach and her students' right to learn. As Mark quiets down, he learns about choices and

A Closer Look

When we assume the best about our students, we see consequences as a way to accelerate their growth.

personal responsibility. And the class has a greater chance to learn content, because disruptions are kept at a minimum.

School is an essential laboratory where students can exercise the muscle of choice at a young age in a relatively safe environment. Although when compared with "real life," consequences in school — such as changing seats or detentions — may seem artificial, they can be gentle practice for students who need to realize the value and impact of their own choices. Later, when they get "on the street," they will be less likely to impulsively steal cars, cut work, or shirk their basic responsibilities of acquiring food, shelter, and human companionship.

When we assume the best about our students, we see consequences as a way to accelerate their growth. This orientation helps us be firm and soft simultaneously, and allows us to move quickly along the continuum of inner authority.

The Nuts and Bolts of Consequences

Now that we've looked at underlying assumptions about consequences, let's get to the nitty-gritty of what to do and how to do it. This section is broken into five main parts: designing consequences, implementing consequences, documenting consequences, making changes in our management systems and extrinsic vs. intrinsic rewards.

Part I. Which consequences to choose

Consequences should be set up in a hierarchy, ranging from a simple reminder to more serious consequences, all of which should:

- ▲ Be natural and/or logical
- ▲ Provide some wiggle room for the teacher
- ▲ Be specific and concrete

Natural/Logical consequences

Consequences are natural or logical if they are appropriately attached to student behaviors. One of the best natural consequences I have ever heard was when a fourteen-year old girl kept slamming the door to her room at home. Her father warned her to stop, and when she didn't, he removed the door from its hinges for a week! That week without privacy was a sufficient reminder to his daughter not to slam her door again! Some examples of natural classroom consequences are:

- ▲ When a student writes on his desk, he has to clean it and perhaps others after school
- ▲ When a student takes up class time with distractions, he has to spend time after class addressing the lessons he avoided
- ▲ When the students stay extra-focused, they earn five to ten minutes of time at the end of class to focus on topics of their choice

Natural/logical consequences allow students to easily make connections between their choices and the consequences that follow. Students can more readily internalize appropriate behavior, and more easily buy into their teacher's management system.

> A fourteen-year old girl kept slamming the door to her room at home. Her father warned her to stop, and when she didn't, he removed the door from its hinges for a week!

Provide some wiggle room for the teacher

Many teachers are concerned about appearing fair to their students. My approach is to let them know that as the teacher, my job is to do what will most help each student learn. Period. Sometimes that differs from student to student and situation to situation. It's our call. Therefore, allowing for a range of consequences for the same rule violations will give us the leeway to make judgment calls, while at the same time being consistent. A simple way to do this is to designate as one of our consequences, "student meets privately with teacher after class." In that meeting we can determine what, if anything, has to happen next. If two students break the same rule, but one student has a legitimate reason, this "leeway clause" allows us to enforce consequences for both, while differentiating between specific situations.

Leeway helps especially if we are using certain consequences for the first time and don't want to set ourselves up for failure by "painting ourselves into a corner." Until we have some experience under our belt, we can't predict exactly how things will go with the consequences we choose. Incorporating leeway allows for some flexibility and responsiveness to situations as they arise. Plus, it gives us time to calm down and consider our options, rather than having to blurt out a decision that we may end up regretting later.

Further, a meeting with the teacher after class allows a student to save face during the moment of conflict. There's time to defuse the tension, get the class on-task, and address consequences later, when the student is more likely ready to learn from the situation, rather than just complain.

Mrs. Allgood says

> Allowing for a range of consequences for the same rule violations will give us the leeway to make judgment calls, while at the same time being consistent.

Finally, when we meet with the student after class, we have the option to give him some options as to what the best consequence should be.

Be specific and concrete

Consequences, like rules, should be behavioral in nature, and clearly delineate actions that students need to take.

What are some possibilities? Every teaching situation is different. So there is no menu I can provide that will work for all teachers. What follows, however, is a simple list of some of the more generic consequences that many teachers have used successfully. Make sure that the consequences you choose mesh well with school and district policies.

Bright Ideas

Examples of Consequences: Four Categories

Category A. reminders and warnings

Nonverbal reminders

- ▲ Teacher pauses.
- ▲ Teacher looks at the student.
- ▲ Teacher gives a "teacher look" to the student.
- ▲ Teacher turns and faces the student, with arms at her side.
- ▲ Teacher walks near the student.
- ▲ Teacher places her hand on the student's desk.
- ▲ Teacher points to the work that the student is supposed to be doing.
- ▲ Teacher gives a nearby student a positive behavior coupon.

Verbal reminders

- ▲ Teacher says the name of the student, either privately or in front of the class.
- ▲ Teacher states the class rule aloud to the class.
- ▲ Teacher comments on other students who are behaving appropriately.

Nonverbal warnings

- ▲ Teacher looks at her timer, signaling that she is about to add time to a class consequence or remove time from a class reward.
- ▲ Teacher removes a post-it note or similar sticker from the student's desk — the student starts with three, and removal of the third means a specific consequence.
- ▲ Teacher picks up a clipboard where she keeps track of individual student behavior.
- ▲ Teacher uses a prearranged hand signal to warn the student.

Bright Ideas

Verbal warnings

▲ Teacher tells the student — either privately or publicly — that, if he continues, a particular consequence will occur.

▲ Teacher says to the student "that's one." At "three," the student knows that a particular consequence will occur.

▲ Teacher lets the class know that its group reward is in jeopardy.

Category B.
Actual consequences inside the classroom

This is one step up from warnings, in that specific and concrete student behaviors result. As above, these consequences can be communicated aloud, in a whisper, or non-verbally, as long as the procedure has been taught in advance.

▲ Teacher asks the student to change seats temporarily.

▲ Teacher asks the student to change seats permanently.

▲ Teacher lowers student's class participation points.

▲ Student is asked to take a time-out from the activity.

▲ Private meeting is arranged between teacher and student, either after class, at lunch, or after school.

▲ Teacher gives an after-school or lunch detention to the student.

▲ Teacher removes a potential group reward, such as extra time at the end of class to focus on a class game or preferred activity.

▲ Teacher removes an individual privilege, such as time spent on the computer.

▲ Teacher gives a nearby student a positive behavior coupon.

▲ Teacher verbally appreciates other well-behaved students.

▲ Teacher verbally appreciates the student when she "catches him being good."

▲ Teacher lets the student know that his parents will be called.

Bright Ideas

▲ Teacher places a referral slip on the student's desk, with the understanding that if the student behaves appropriately until class is over, he can tear up the slip.

▲ Student is asked to flip a color card on the class chart on the wall. Each student's day starts green, and can go to yellow or red. Each color corresponds to specific rewards or consequences.

▲ Student is asked to check a box on his behavior card, and place it in the slot on the wall. This is similar to color cards, except that the behavior card has check boxes that delineate the particular infraction. A blank slot means no infractions. A white card means one infraction. A pink card means a second infraction. (For more on card systems, check this chapter's section called "Documenting Misbehavior.")

Category C.
When a student is removed from the classroom

This is a separate category for three reasons. First, it means that the student will lose instructional time. Second, it involves other school personnel. And third, it guarantees that the student in question will no longer be disrupting class, at least while he's gone. It tends to have at least a temporary quieting impact on the rest of the students.

▲ Student takes a time-out in the hall.

▲ Student takes a time-out on the school designated time-out bench.

▲ Student is sent to another teacher's classroom. This is generally an underutilized consequence that can be very effective, especially if the student is sent to a classroom of students who are significantly younger or older than he is. One way to do it is to send a referral slip with the student to the other class. The receiving teacher knows that the student

Bright Ideas

is bordering on being sent to the office, and that any disruption whatsoever will get that result. It helps to give the student an assignment to work on silently in the new class.

▲ Student sent to the office for a variety of consequences, including

   ▲ Referrals

   ▲ Detentions

   ▲ Lunch detail

   ▲ Parent/guardian conferences

   ▲ Suspensions

   ▲ Expulsions

Category D. "Behind-the-scenes" efforts

This is a key element of invisible classroom management. Mrs. Meanswell might not observe Mrs. Allgood talking privately with or about her student, but these conversations can make all the difference in the world. Personal contact with the student, his parents, counselors, and other teachers can provide the glue to make desired changes stick.

▲ Teacher talks with student privately outside of class time. Often this can take the form of a structured pep talk, although it can also be more focused on the consequences that the student is incurring and the behaviors that need to change. The combination of firm and soft in this meeting can do the trick. Getting to know the student and asking him to volunteer solutions to his behavior problems can also be quite effective. This is explained in more detail in Chapter 13, "Breaking the Cycle of Student Misbehavior."

Bright Ideas

- ▲ Teacher talks with the student's counselor, the principal, other teachers, to gain information that may be helpful in addressing the student's behavior and/or emotional needs.
- ▲ Teacher talks with parent(s) about student's misbehavior. When this works, it works incredibly well, as word spreads and one call affects several kids. It is often the first thing that the teacher should do when a student is beginning to show signs of being out of control.
- ▲ Teacher talks with parents to commend student behavior. An underutilized strategy that often bears tremendous fruit. A variation is to call the student at home in the evening and let him know how improved his behavior is. Naturally, his parents will be informed of the call. If they don't believe their child, then when they call the teacher to check up, it's a golden opportunity to speak with the parents in a positive way about their child, and invite the parents to come in for a conference.
- ▲ Parent conferences at school with the principal, the counselor, and other teachers, with or without the student. This classic model reflects to the student how he is behaving in all his classes and keeps the student from claiming that one particular teacher has it out for him.
- ▲ Individual behavior contracts between the student and the teacher, ideally focusing on only one behavior at a time. These are described in detail in Chapter 13 "Breaking the Cycle of Student Misbehavior" on page 212.
- ▲ Teacher has positive contact with the student outside of class. This could consist of simply watching him perform in a school play or soccer game.

Student Choice

It helps to frame all consequences around the student's choices. For example, "Mark, the rule in this class is that we listen attentively when others are speaking. You have chosen to talk out of turn, and therefore need to meet with me after class."

Student participation in rules and/or consequences

Many teachers give their students some input in designing rules and consequences. When students do participate, they tend to have a buy-in and are more likely to adhere to the rules and not argue with the consequences when they receive them. This approach works as long as teachers are comfortable with it; if we don't buy into it, it won't fly.

Student input can take many forms, ranging from full to quasi-democratic participation. One way I've done it allows me to decide late in the game how much say I want my students to have. Without telling them why, I ask students to brainstorm characteristics of a good teacher and characteristics of a good student. They can do this for homework or in class, alone or in groups. Then I collect and type up the characteristics most commonly listed — usually about ten characteristics for both the teacher and the student. These then become the guidelines for the class, which can be used as the basis for generating specific rules and consequences, or not. Part of it depends on what they've come up with. It's up to me. And, because I collate the characteristics, I can weed out those that I can't live with. One thing to note is that the guidelines students generate for themselves are usually tighter than we could ever get away with. Also, guidelines for the teacher are almost always sensible and valid, and often include, "The teacher will be fair," "The teacher won't yell unless absolutely necessary," or "The teacher will be available after school to help students with their homework."

Mrs. Allgood says

Giving students tailored options can help them buy into the process while helping them see us as on their side, even as we enforce the rules.

This technique can be modified to fit our comfort level. For example, we could generate some of the rules, and have the students generate the others. We could generate the rules ourselves, and have the students help generate some of the consequences for specific rule violations. Or we could make up the rules and consequences ourselves, but give students consequence options at the point in time when they break the rules. For example, "Sally, you didn't hand in your homework. You now have two choices: you can work on it during recess; or you can work on it after school." Or, "Mark, you were writing on your desk again. You can either stay after school and clean the desks in the room, or pick up trash around the campus for twenty minutes." Giving students tailored options can help them buy into the process while helping them see us as on their side, even as we enforce the rules.

Another element in involving students is to have them think and talk meta-cognitively about rules and consequences. We can ask them why societies (and classrooms) have rules, and to identify situations where consequences are needed. It will help them increase their ownership and support of the system that gets set up in our classroom.

Quizzing students on rules and consequences

It's not enough to come up with a discipline plan, whether or not students have some say in its design. Just as in teaching content, the plan needs to be taught. Let's discuss our principles, rules and consequences with our students, breaking each element down and teaching its parts. We can check for understanding in a number of ways, including a quiz or test. Classroom management consultant Rick Curwin suggests making sure that every student takes the test and that every student gets 100% on it. If a student fails, he can take it again until he gets 100%.

Teachers should keep copies of these quizzes. If during the school year a student claims he didn't know the rule, or wasn't aware of the consequences, he can be referred to the quiz that he aced at the beginning of the year. This same quiz can be used when we meet with parents about their child's behavior.

▲ ▲ ▲

Part 2. Implementing consequences

Always implement consequences

Even if we use only a nonverbal reminder in a given situation, this helps establish the rules as rules, not just whims. When Mrs. Meanswell ignores inappropriate behavior, the students see her "asleep at the wheel." When Mrs. Allgood notices infractions by giving gentle reminders, her students see her as the "bestower of grace" in the classroom. Consistency in implementing consequences may be difficult at first, but it sends a clear message to students that we are willing to receive the charge of being in charge. And this will assure them that they are in the right room for learning behavior, and thus don't have to act out to see if we are the right teacher for them.

Go from mild to strict

Mrs. Allgood always starts with the mildest consequence first. If that doesn't work, she increases the
impact of the consequence slightly. She doesn't jump
from "reminder" to "suspension." This is for two reasons: first, it isn't fair to the student, because then the
consequence is being used as a punishment rather than a
teaching tool. Second, it isn't fair to her, because the gray
area between the two consequences is so extreme, she'll
be hesitant to use the second consequence. Many Mrs.
Meanswells box themselves in with systems that demand
harshness. I call this "the Picket Fence Syndrome,"
where a teacher has too many pickets missing in her
"fence" of consequences. We are not here to be punitive,
but to provide a pause during which the student can
reassess his choices. If he continues to make a choice that
disrupts the class or his learning, then we choose another consequence, another pause. A repetition of the first consequence won't
serve to pause him the second time; we need something slightly
more impactful.

A Closer Look

When Mrs. Meanswell ignores inappropriate behavior, the students see her "asleep at the wheel." When Mrs. Allgood notices infractions by giving gentle reminders, her students see her as the "bestower of grace" in the classroom.

Our job is simply to act as a go-between or liaison, connecting
students with the consequences they choose. We deliver the consequences as gently as we can, but deliver them we must. Ideally,
the student will recognize his responsibility, rather than perceiving
the teacher as the one who has made the tough decision.

Justifying consequence implementation

If many students are talking out of turn, how do we
decide which one to address with consequences? How
do we justify our decision to the student? One answer:
When all the cars are speeding on the same stretch of
road, what does the highway patrol officer say when
she pulls over only one car for going ten miles over the
speed limit? "Take care of your own driving, and you

A Closer Look

We are not here to be punitive, but to provide a pause during which the student can reassess his choices.

won't have to worry about what does or doesn't happen to the other drivers on the road."

Students are here to learn the value of free will. The more we can connect their behaviors to their choices, and provide them a sense of responsibility, the better off they'll be in the long run.

Let our consequences do the talking

We can lecture all we want about appropriate behavior. We can reason, appeal to students' sense of morality, whatever. This will work with most students for anywhere from thirty seconds to several minutes. However, using a consequence, delivered without animosity, will better hold our students' attention and reinforce what we're talking about. This means that we don't have to raise our voices, threaten, act mean, react, apologize, hide our heads in the sand, or scold. We can simply, gently, and firmly enforce the consequence, while internally remembering that we're on the same side as the student, and that he wants to learn behavior.

A Closer Look

In ranting at Mark, Mrs. Meanswell is communicating her own weakness.

Let's say Mark has been quite disruptive, and needs to stay after class. Mrs. Meanswell says, "Mark! I'm sick and tired of your attitude. I have warned you and warned you, and you still don't listen. You need to stay after school today. No ifs, ands, or buts. I'm not going to tolerate your misbehavior anymore."

What Mark actually hears is: "Mark! Blah blah blah blah after school blah blah blah." The subtext of what he hears is, "I am so frustrated that I don't have any control here, I'm getting angry and flustered." In ranting at Mark, Mrs. Meanswell is communicating her own weakness.

The alternative? A more Allgood-like response: "Mark. Please meet with me after school." The consequence itself does the work, and Mrs. Allgood communicates her strength rather than her weakness. As long as Mark knows that Mrs. Allgood means business, she can communicate the consequence in as mild or matter-of-fact tone as she wants.

Both Mrs. Meanswell and Mrs. Allgood want their students to learn morals and values. Mrs. Meanswell tends to focus on values in the heat of the moment when her students are caught misbehaving. Mrs. Allgood addresses them when her students are more receptive, in class lessons before misbehaviors occur, and after misbehaving students have had a chance to calm down.

Volume

Teachers almost never have to raise their voices unless it's fun. Ultimately, teacher yelling, displeasure, and anger are tiring and tiresome consequences. Students often bristle when we yell. If yelling at our students is habitual, we may "win each battle," but we'll end up creating a war. Ultimately, we'll find ourselves coming to work each day readying for battle, rather than anticipating the wonder that can come from teaching and learning. If we find ourselves yelling more than we want to, it's usually a signal that our management system has a loophole that needs addressing. In fact, many teachers discover that on days when they lose their voice and have to whisper, the noise level in the room goes down dramatically!

A Closer Look

Mrs. Meanswell tends to focus on values when her students are caught misbehaving. Mrs. Allgood addresses values when her students are more receptive.

There is a big difference between yelling *at* students and yelling *to* them. Unfortunately, students don't always recognize the difference. P.E. teachers, for example, often yell across the field to get students' attention. Yet some students take it the wrong way. The solution in P.E. is to do what we can to avoid yelling, including using a whistle or other sound signal, teaching the procedures as clearly as possible in advance, and assigning student leaders to communicate messages to students across the field.

Catch students doing well

Consequences are not just for inappropriate behavior. They are also equally valid for appropriate and/or exemplary behavior. We need to let students know when they are succeeding. This will help them appreciate their choices and learn responsibility.

Generally speaking, most young students like public praise and appreciation. With older students, it's sometimes better to speak to them privately. One benefit of public appreciation is that other students tend to be motivated as well.

Student behavior during independent work

When students are working on their own or in small groups, and we are circulating from student to student, how do we guide them into keeping their focus and staying on task? Try the following three steps, as suggested by classroom management consultant Fred Jones:

▲ Tell them one thing they are doing that's working.
▲ Tell them the next thing they need to do.
▲ Move on to the next student.

It backfires to get hooked into long conversations. We have too many students for that. Plus, they need to learn independent work skills. Foster this with quick spot-checks and reminders.

If a student is not on task, try some nonverbal strategies. Turn to face the student. Look at him. Pause. Then look at the work, and if necessary, point to it. Pause again. Make sure to "hang around" for a few extra seconds to see that the student is actually working, and not just appearing to work.

If nonverbal strategies don't work, try these three questions:

▲ What are you doing?
▲ What should you be doing?
▲ What are you going to do now?

Again, we don't need to buy into all the excuses and explanations. We can address the behavior, put the responsibility on to the student, and move on.

Here's yet another strategy. If a student is misbehaving, ask him one or more of these three questions regarding his behavior:

▲ Is it safe?
▲ Is it kind?
▲ Is it productive?

This strategy works best for younger students, but variations can be tailored for older students.

Chaos at the end of class

Mrs. Allgood says

We don't need to buy into all the excuses and explanations. We can address the behavior, put the responsibility on to the student, and move on.

Ah, that really rowdy moment just before class ends — what teacher hasn't experienced it? Perhaps kids put their backpacks on and gather around the door, waiting for the bell to ring. Certainly a teacher can elbow through the crowd, block the doorway, and command students to return to their desks while being chastised for charging the door. Inevitably, during the speech, the bell will have rung and the students will quite possibly be complaining that they are missing their break or have to go.

While ideally it's good to "nip such behavior in the bud," there's nothing wrong with waiting until we next see students to talk to them about appropriate behavior — and then mete out any necessary consequences. If there's only one minute left and we've already "lost them," we don't necessarily need to "reel them in." Until next time.

Tailor kids' choices

Never give kids choices about anything unless we are willing to follow through with whatever choices they make. When I student-taught my ninth-grade class-from-heck, the one with Phil the Baiter, I remember introducing a new management system in the middle of the semester. I introduced a timer to calculate off-task time, and told students that if their behavior improved to a certain point, they would receive a reward in the form of a movie of their choice. When they finally earned their reward, their top two choices for movies were *Debbie Does Dallas* and *The Texas Chain Saw Massacre*! Needless to say, I couldn't let them watch either, and had to face an uprising of incensed youth who demanded they get what I had promised them.

The more we can anticipate worst-case scenarios, the more proactive we can be in successfully — and peacefully — tailoring student options.

Sending students to the office

Teachers are often concerned about sending students out of the classroom. They believe that they will be perceived by the administration as weak or incompetent if their students appear in the office. Granted, it's not a good habit to send students out for slight reasons, but there are plenty of situations where it is a perfectly suitable option. In these situations, it can ease the teacher's mind if she sets up a meeting with the administrator in advance of sending a student out. Let the administrator know that Mark has been particularly off-the-wall lately, and ask, "Would it be okay if I sent him out of class if it happens again?" ("What time would be best for you? Okay, I can pencil in a meeting with Mark at 10:30...."). This places the administrator where she should be — working with the teacher — and removes most of the teacher's anxiety about being judged as weak.

A Closer Look

Sometimes administrators and teachers have different definitions of "support."

This strategy also works well with teachers whose administrators are inconsistent in their support. By setting up the meeting between the student and the administrator in advance, the administrator is much less likely to send the student back to the classroom after just a few minutes.

Also, sometimes administrators and teachers have different definitions of "support." It's a good idea to clarify exactly what the administrator thinks her role is, and exactly what we think we need, thus narrowing the gap between the two definitions, and likely increasing the support we will receive. This clarification can be done directly, or through conversations with a mentor teacher, if a new teacher is particularly concerned about how the administration might perceive her.

Let students save face

It is often a good idea to delay consequences and/or talk privately with students. If a student feels cornered, he will most likely do anything he can to get out of the corner, including increasing the level of conflict. On occasion, then, there's nothing wrong with giving him the last word, if it can help de-escalate tension.

We don't have to give consequences right away. We can get the misbehaving student quiet, refocus the class, and talk to that student later about his consequence. As long as we implement the consequence at some point during or after class, the consequence will do the talking. Students in the class will ultimately get the message that we are willing to hold our ground. Plus, we'll be able to sidestep some confrontations that would inevitably occur if we challenged the student in the heat of the moment.

Mrs. Allgood says

We don't have to give consequences right away. We can get the misbehaving student quiet, refocus the class, and talk to that student later about his consequence.

Whenever possible, we should communicate with our students privately. This helps students save face in front of their peers, which can go a long way in diffusing tension. When we do talk with students in front of their peers, it helps to assume the best about them and speak in a calm and respectful voice.

For example, Mark is fidgeting and distracting the students around him. Here are two possible teacher responses:

Mrs. Meanswell (from across the room):
"Mark! I warned you and you still haven't stopped. You're staying after school today!"

Mark: "What! No way! I wasn't talking! Why do you always pick on me?!..."

| Mrs. Allgood | (walks up to Mark and whispers to him): "Hi Mark. I see you're having a hard time today. Why don't you see if you can focus for the next ten minutes, and then you and I can talk privately after the activity and see if we can't find a way to make the rest of your day go better." |
| Mark: | "Okay, I'll try…" |

Afterward, Mrs. Allgood can let Mark know how much she appreciates his willingness to refocus. She can also ask Mark to stay after school as a consequence for his initial disruption. He's much less likely to argue with her and much more likely to show up after school because of the following lessons:

A Closer Look

> When we treat students with dignity, they are more likely to respond in dignified ways.

- ▲ He's had a chance to calm down,
- ▲ He wasn't cornered publicly by Mrs. Allgood, and
- ▲ He doesn't have an audience.

When we treat students with dignity, they are more likely to respond in dignified ways.

Choose consequences we feel comfortable using

Mrs. Meanswell might have a great looking hierarchy of consequences, but she avoids using one or two key consequences because she isn't comfortable with them. For example, one consequence is that she will call parents, yet she doesn't call them. Perhaps she is intimidated, she doesn't see the value in it, or it simply takes too much time and energy. It doesn't matter that Mrs. Allgood, down the hall, calls parents. Mrs. Meanswell has to either be willing to call, or find and use other consequences that will work better for her.

Appreciation for physical education teachers

P.E. is, I believe, one of the hardest types of classes to manage, for several reasons:

- ▲ P.E. teachers have larger classes
- ▲ They have either no classroom at all (the field) or a room with multiple exit doors (the gymnasium)
- ▲ Some students tend to take P.E. less seriously than their other classes
- ▲ Some use P.E. to go overboard with energy expenditure
- ▲ Many students find the very nature of P.E. to be humiliating, and thus act out all the more

In addition to P.E., classes like home economics, woodshop and autoshop can be quite challenging, especially for beginning teachers. Perhaps the most challenging class to manage is "Beginning Band." Sixty kids with noisemakers — whose idea was that?

▲ ▲ ▲

Part 3. Documenting misbehavior

Many teachers use check marks on their roll sheets or in their grade books to record inappropriate behavior. The drawback to this is that there are many different types of inappropriate behaviors. If we don't know the details, then we can't recognize patterns, and have less ability to help teach our students to turn things around. Further, documenting the specifics helps when talking with parents, counselors, and other teachers. If students have a section on their report cards for behavior (usually in the elementary grades), then having specifics at our fingertips can be quite helpful.

The "ADOPT" system

A simple solution is to use an acronym to describe the particular categories of behaviors we want to document. Classroom management consultant Rick Morris has developed a system called "Adopt:"

Perhaps the most challenging class to manage is "Beginning Band." Sixty kids with noisemakers — whose idea was that?

Not Paying **A**ttention
Not following **D**irections
Being **O**ff-task
Playing around
Not turning in assignments on **T**ime

This system makes use of a class-seating chart for each class we teach. When a student misbehaves, we write on the chart the letter of the acronym that corresponds to the misbehavior. We can later transfer the information to forms that go home to parents and into our computer-grading program.

We can use the ADOPT acronym, or choose whatever letters make sense in our classroom. For example, an "S" could be used when a student gets out of his seat, a "C" for calling out, and a "D" for disrupting class.

Record keeping systems are not consequence systems. They may help keep track of trends in student misbehaviors, but for the most part they don't change those behaviors. The exception is that every time the teacher goes to write on her clipboard, students tend to temporarily behave better. But if she relies solely on using the threat of writing on the clipboard to manage student behavior, it will wear out very quickly. Concrete consequences need to be implemented on a consistent basis.

Using a card system

Elementary teachers can set up part of a bulletin board for cards of three to five different colors, depending on the system. Each student has a pocket on the board with a card in it. For example, a green card means that the student is behaving appropriately. Yellow stands for a warning. Peach means the student was warned once, then broke another rule and has earned consequence number one. A blue card stands for two broken rules and consequence number two. Of course, specific consequences are up to the teacher and her design.

There are several advantages to this system:

A Closer Look

Record keeping systems are not consequence systems.

- ▲ The students have to flip their own cards, thus kinesthetically connecting to their behavior, and saving the teacher the time and distraction.
- ▲ The students can monitor where they are behaviorally.
- ▲ The teacher can see where the students are behaviorally.

There are several disadvantages to this system:

- ▲ It doesn't distinguish between types of misbehavior, although this can be addressed in the gradebook or clip-board.
- ▲ It publicizes student misbehaviors, thus potentially embarrassing students.
- ▲ The teacher can sometimes mistake it for the actual implementation of consequences.

▲ ▲ ▲

Part 4. Making changes in our system

Some teachers believe that if they don't start out the school year "on the right track," they are doomed for the rest of the school year. This isn't true. Any time we want to revamp our management system, we can. If we are concerned about what to say to our students, let's tell them the truth: "Class, it's been getting a little noisy lately, so we're going to try a new system." When I student-taught my ninth-grade English class-from-heck, it seemed like every two weeks I introduced "Mr. Smith's new classroom management policy."

If we change our system in the middle of the school year, it may take longer than we think to see if it is working. When a captain wants to turn her moving ship, she first has to slow down, then shift directions, and then regain her original speed. The most vulnerable capsize point is after slowing down — just at the point of turning. And the point when a change in our management system is most likely to elicit chaos is often three or four days after its implementation. We should give any major policy shift at least two weeks, ten school days, before deciding whether it is working. Success is more likely if we stick to our new policy consistently and remain patient. Remember, it takes us time to adjust — and our students even more time.

Wise Apple Advice

> We should give any major policy shift at least two weeks, ten school days, before deciding whether it's working.

Implementation — one step at a time

I used to have a hard time making changes in my classroom. I'd leave a staff development workshop inspired to make seventeen different changes right away. But then I'd hit the wall. "Oh, I can't do it this week because we've got Back to School night. Next week we've got a special field trip. The week after that progress reports are due. Then we've got a special assembly, final exams, and parent meetings." After six weeks, I found that I hadn't implemented anything, and it was time for a new staff development workshop. The old information would be shelved for the new information, which would go through the same process of inspiration and non-implementation.

I finally came up with a formula for making changes that has helped me immensely:

▲ I make a list of changes I want to make, putting them in priority order.
▲ I make sure that number one is doable. If it's too complicated, I break it up into smaller steps, assigning a number to each step.
▲ I always implement number one only.
▲ I start with my favorite class. It's the one that's most forgiving. If I teach elementary, then I start only on Fridays,

or only in social studies, or only when the science kids rotate to my classroom.

▲ After the change is working with my favorite class, I introduce it to the rest of my classes.

▲ Once it is solid in all my classes, I start the process over with a new number one.

Teachers learn just like students learn — one step at a time. By slowing down my agenda for change, I find that I actually make more permanent changes more quickly. Teachers are so busy that to make wholesale changes can seem overwhelming and intimidating. That's why one small step at a time works. We are scientists, and our classroom is our lab. By starting small with one class or situation, we can control the experiment more, and are more likely to follow through. We make our mistakes, learn on the job, and gain confidence in a relatively controlled and safe environment, just like our students.

Mrs. Allgood says

> We are scientists, and our classroom is our lab. By starting small with one class or situation, we can control the experiment more, and are more likely to follow through.

How to introduce a group incentive

Students are more likely to work hard for a group incentive, such as a twenty-minute educational game on Friday, if they first have a "free taste" of the incentive. After they've tasted it through a short exposure to the game, they can be required to earn it the next time through appropriate behavior, such as all students being on time to class, or transition times kept below a certain maximum. An additional approach is to make the criterion for success fairly simple the first couple of times, so the students see the connection between their positive behavior and the incentive that they receive. Once they have bought-in to trying to earn the incentive, the teacher can make the criteria more challenging.

▲ ▲ ▲

Part 5. Extrinsic vs. intrinsic rewards

Some people think extrinsic rewards are **training wheels**, temporary motivators that allow students to form positive behavioral habits; once habits are learned, the rewards are discarded from the equation. Others think extrinsic rewards are **crutches** that rely on an external locus of control, one that disables students' natural motivation to participate, learn, and cooperate. The end result of extrinsic rewards, so the crutch argument goes, is that before engaging in an activity, students increasingly need to know "What's this worth?" or "Does this count?"

Many suggest that extrinsic rewards do work for the short term, but eventually lose their power to motivate. Over time, students tend to become numb to them.

Where do I stand in the argument? Somewhere in the middle. I have seen initially motivating rewards slowly lose their luster, and I've watched many Mrs. Allgoods who successfully use reward systems. Overall, I believe it's ideal if teachers can motivate students intrinsically, but there are many times, especially in the beginning of their careers, when teachers need to use strategies that work right away, regardless of the long-term issues.

> That old adage, "Give a person a fish and she eats for a day, but teach her to fish and she eats for a lifetime," didn't apply to me. When I was a new teacher, I would have starved to death while learning to fish. I needed fish immediately.

That old adage, "Give a person a fish and she eats for a day, but teach her to fish and she eats for a lifetime," didn't apply to me. When I was a new teacher, I would have starved to death while learning to fish. I needed fish immediately, so I took whatever I could get. Later on, as I became a better classroom manager, I was able to rely less and less on rewards or consequences to keep my students focused. This can often trip up Mrs. Meanswell, because she watches how Mrs. Allgood does it and tries the exact same style. But Mrs. Allgood has spent years learning and practicing how to intrinsically motivate her students.

When using rewards, I suggest that teachers be conscious of the potential long-term limitations and pitfalls. Counterbalance them with a lot of genuine appreciation of students, as well as individual conversations with them geared toward fostering intrinsic motivation.

Further, some rewards are more natural than others. For example, if students keep class transition times to a minimum, giving them candy would be an artificial reward. Giving them time at the end of class to do their homework would be more natural — since they saved time to earn time. The more natural the incentive, the more the students are likely to internalize their motivation.

Appreciation vs. praise

The difference between appreciation and praise, as I see it, is that appreciation is genuine, whereas praise is mechanical.

Praise acts like an addictive drug. Students respond to it positively at first, but then either become immune to it or need increasing doses to be affected. It works to motivate students initially, but the value of praise recedes over time.

Appreciation, on the other hand, does not fade. As teachers, if we are genuine in expressing what we appreciate about our students, then we make and reinforce a personal connection with them. Like all human beings, they are hungry for genuine personal connections. Appreciation addresses that hunger and can positively nurture our students without ever running out of steam or seeming false. It is the "gift that keeps on giving."

There is a place in the classroom for praising students, and in the short run, it generally does work to motivate them. That "short run" may last the whole school year for some. If we are genuine, however, our students will receive a much more powerful message, and will tend to internalize an appreciation of themselves rather than a need for external compliments.

> **A Closer Look**
>
> Praise acts like an addictive drug. Students respond to it positively at first, but then either become immune to it or need increasing doses to be affected. Appreciation, on the other hand, is the gift that keeps giving.

Gifts vs. rewards

Rewards are prizes — food, stuff, free time — offered by the teacher as an incentive for students to behave well. The students know in advance what they can earn with appropriate or exemplary behavior. Gifts, on the other hand, are spontaneous in nature, coming as appreciation for positive behavior that has already happened.

For example, if Mrs. Allgood uses a timer to track instructional time lost due to student misbehavior, and tells her students they can have a popcorn party on Friday if they stay on task during transitions throughout the week, then she is offering them a reward for their behavior. If, on the other hand, on Friday she announces to the students that they have done so well with transitions throughout the week that she wants to throw them a popcorn party, then she is giving them a gift.

The main difference is that rewards are used as an extrinsic form of motivation, whereas gifts are an intrinsic expression of appreciation.

Wise Apple Advice

A final reminder about consequences

Most of Mrs. Allgood's classroom management is focused on prevention. Consequences are intervention. As Mrs. Meanswell increases her inner authority and her ability to teach procedures, maintain consistency, and establish positive connections with her students, she'll find herself needing consequences less and less.

DOG TRAINING SCHOOL
(Homework Excuse #1)

13

BREAKING THE CYCLE OF STUDENT MISBEHAVIOR

> *"When the going gets tough,*
> *the tough get supportive."*

F OR PARTICULARLY TOUGH KIDS and situations, employing all the approaches outlined in previous chapters doesn't do the trick. Even with the use of heavy-duty consequences, some kids continue to break the rules. What then? How do we help our students make permanent positive changes? While there are no guaranteed solutions, the most effective approaches arise out of our tried-and-true combination of assuming the best and breaking things into parts, as shown in all the strategies described below.

Assumptions that Make a Difference

Addressing the causes

To get to the root of student misbehaviors, we may need to address the reasons behind them. This doesn't always seem practical, given the limited time we have. But it can make all the difference.

Bright Ideas

Why students act out

▲ When they don't understand the lesson, they may choose to push away feeling inadequate. They'd much rather see themselves as behavior problems than slow learners.

▲ They feel frustrated because they don't get it, and rather than treat frustration as a doorway into learning, they push it away, and end up acting out.

▲ It's possible that the lesson is inappropriate for them, and they act out as a communication to the teacher to change the lesson or the approach.

▲ It's possible that the behavior the teacher expects is unrealistic.

▲ The teacher has been reacting at them rather than responding with them.

▲ They are having problems at home.

▲ They are using drugs. Although drug use is often viewed as a symptom of underlying problems, once done with regularity, drugs can become the problem.

▲ They are having trouble with medication — not taking it, taking it too much, or not taking it regularly.

▲ They have emotional tension with peers.

▲ They are being bullied and/or intimidated by classmates.

▲ They are struggling in other classes.

▲ A myriad of other reasons, both in and out of the classroom.

Students don't act out because they are bad people. They are simply looking for ways to establish and maintain a sense of self while navigating through the sometimes extreme experiences they have. When a student acts out, it is often a call for help. By addressing these calls directly and honing in on solutions, we provide students with a chance to make real and lasting changes. If in our investigation we discover reasons beyond our control, we can at least gain compassion for our students and ourselves, knowing what can and can't be changed.

Helpful approaches

Positive connections

Talking with Mark about his life requires that the teacher establish strong positive connections with him. Many strategies for this are outlined in Chapter 7, "Positive Connections." The essence of all the strategies is simply to talk with him — not about his poor behavior, but about anything he's interested in. Give him a chance to have personal time with us when we are not playing the role of authoritarian. Make this an ongoing commitment. It won't be easy, especially at first. He'll likely be wary of our sudden interest in his life. But if we stick with it, casually and consistently over the course of days — not as a one-time frontal assault — we'll notice that gradually Mark becomes more forthcoming, more involved, and more committed to succeeding in the class.

A Closer Look

When a student acts out, it is often a call for help. By addressing these calls directly and honing in on solutions, we provide students with a chance to make real and lasting changes.

"I-Statements" and active listening

Students like Mark want to feel respected and heard. One way is for the teacher to make an effort to listen closely and fully to what he has to say. It helps to repeat back to him what we hear, to make sure the communication is clear. For example, "I hear you saying that you think it's unfair that I singled you out when others were talking as well."

Mrs. Allgood says

Give students a chance to have personal time with us when we are not playing the role of authoritarian.

It also helps to make statements about ourselves, using the word "I." An example would be, "I feel concerned when I give the class a direction and you come up right afterwards to ask me what it was." I-statements help disarm situations. Because we are not directly making claims about Mark, he won't be as inclined to want to defend himself.

Listening is powerful. It's often enough to help the student turn around. If not, it can help us figure out the cause of the problem, giving us a chance to find simple solutions.

If students are hungry, sometimes the best thing we can do is to feed them

If students keep calling out for attention, let's find ways to give it to them that assist the class, rather than disrupt it. We can give classroom jobs to our students; they can be in charge of supplies, pets and plants, collecting and/or passing out papers, designing bulletin boards, taking messages to other teachers, record keeping, welcoming new students, orientating other students to the computer. We can involve them in teaching their peers or teaching younger students from other classes.

Mrs. Allgood says

If students keep calling out for attention, let's find ways to give it to them that assist the class, rather than disrupt it.

If students are fidgety and feel the need to move, let's provide them with the opportunity. Consultant Alan Mendler suggests that teachers use bungee cords or surgical elastic for ADHD kids. Tie lengths around the four legs of the students' chair, so that they can push against them with their legs. Above the chair, the teacher will see model students, still and focused on the lesson. Below the chair will be student legs moving at a hundred miles an hour. We can build movement into our lessons, by periodically providing students with squeeze-toys or art supplies, or sending them on errands. As we assume that students want to learn, let's also assume that sometimes they just need to move.

Five Keys for Permanent Change

Sometimes knowing why doesn't help. Other times we can't figure out why. What then? Permanently changing behavior is not easy, for kids or adults — just think of all the time, money, and energy adults spend on losing weight and quitting smoking. Nonetheless, in the classroom there are some approaches that do seem to make a difference in student behavior. All permanent change involves one or more of the five keys described below (the first three echo consultant Rick Curwin). Students have to:

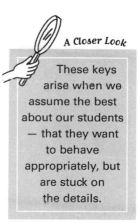

A Closer Look

These keys arise when we assume the best about our students — that they want to behave appropriately, but are stuck on the details.

1. **Want** to change
2. Know **how** to change
3. Have opportunities to **practice** changing
4. Be **conscious** of their choices as they are choosing them
5. Receive ongoing **support** from the teacher

These keys arise when we assume the best about our students — that they want to behave appropriately, but are stuck on the details. Below are three examples that help illustrate how these keys can be used to help our students.

Example 1. Elementary school

Mrs. Allgood teaches a second grade class and her student Johnny has a terrible time with transitions. During the long-term art project, he is always the last one to put his materials away and return his chair to where it belongs. She's tried everything to get him to succeed. She's even tried a group reward if the whole class cleaned up in a given time. But Johnny still didn't do it fast enough, and the whole class suffered. What can she do? She assumes the best about Johnny — that he does want to learn this behavior. She assumes that for whatever reason, it's too complex for him. All her pep talks work for too short a time. He gets distracted and loses momentum.

Her solution is to break up his required task into smaller pieces. She talks to Johnny after school about what her expectations are. She gets him to buy-in that **he wants to make a change.** She then clarifies how he can succeed. When no one else is in the room, she puts the art supplies on his desk and sits him down. She asks him where the supplies need to go when it's time to clean up (**how**). She then has him **practice** putting the supplies away. She asks him to talk about the distractions that occur during class, and what he can do to counter them (**conscious of his choices**). **She supports him** by encouraging him to succeed the next day during class.

A Closer Look

She gives Johnny the *minimum amount of support* he needs to ensure that he succeeds completely.

The next day, just before the students begin to put their art supplies away, Mrs. Allgood has a brief, private conversation with Johnny, reminding him of what they did after school the day before. "Johnny, remember our talk about cleaning up the art materials? What are you going to do with the scissors? Where does this paper go? How about the markers? Do you think you can do this? You know what, I know you can. I'm going to stand right next to you when the class starts cleaning up, so you can show me how well you can do it. I'm about to ask the class to clean up. Are you ready?" Then she announces to the class that it's time to put the supplies away. Then she gives Johnny the *minimum amount of support* he needs to ensure that he succeeds completely. In Johnny's case, it might initially mean that Mrs. Allgood walks him from station to station, handing him the supplies one at a time, and encouraging him as he goes. In content teaching, this is called "guided practice." It's the same in teaching procedures or behavior. When he's completed the task, she lets him know how well he did.

The following day, she does the same thing. On the third day, she pulls back a bit. She tells Johnny, "You've done so well the last two days putting your art supplies away, this time when I ask the class to clean up, I'm going to stand in the back of the room and watch how well you do." If this is too big a step for Johnny to succeed, she comes up with an intermediary step: "Johnny, this time

A Closer Look

Mrs. Allgood is therefore not only Johnny's "imparter of content," she is also his coach and cheerleader.

I'm going to stand in the back and watch how well you can put things away. Each time you put an item away, please stop and look at me, and give me a thumbs up. I'll give you a thumbs up, and then you can go on to the next station." Over time, Mrs. Allgood pulls back more and more. At some point Johnny will have internalized the appropriate behavior, and will be able to put his supplies away without needing her extra guidance.

The support Mrs. Allgood provides makes a big difference. Her actively assuming the best about him is contagious; he starts to assume the best about himself. He starts wanting to change and is more willing to try. Mrs. Allgood is therefore not only Johnny's "imparter of content," she is also his coach and cheerleader.

Example 2. Middle school

Josh is a sixth-grade student who constantly disrupts class by calling out of turn. Consequences haven't made a difference, because he's essentially unaware that he's doing it. Before consequences have any power, he needs to slow down internally to the point where is he aware of his choice to call out as he's making it.

His teacher, Mrs. Allgood, has a conversation with Josh after school. First, she gets him to agree that it's in his best interest to change his behavior. The conversation continues:

Mrs. Allgood:	Josh, if you tried really hard not to call out in class tomorrow, how many times would you call out?
Josh:	None! I promise I'll never do it again!
Mrs. Allgood:	I appreciate your desire, Josh, but calling out can be a hard habit to break, even if you try really hard. Today in class you probably called out ten or more times. What do you think would be a more realistic number, if you tried really hard?
Josh:	Hmm. Maybe… three times?
Mrs. Allgood:	That seems like a more realistic goal. I'll tell you what. Tomorrow when class starts, I'll put four yellow post-it notes on your desk. Each time you call out, I'll give you a private hand signal, by touching my ear like this. Your job when you call out is to remove one note, crumple it up, and put it in your pocket. Let's see if you can have at least one note remaining by the time class ends.

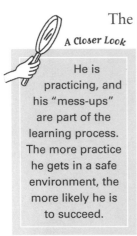

The next day, Josh does his best to abide by the new policy. He is now kinesthetically monitoring his own progress, slowing down internally, and increasing his awareness of his choice to call out. What happens if he uses up all four post-it notes with twenty minutes to go in class? Should Mrs. Allgood give him a consequence? Not initially. It would help him more if she simply gave him more notes, and encouraged him to do better the next time (Kindergarten kids who sit on the floor can put bracelets around their wrists instead of post-it notes on their desks). He is practicing, and his "mess-ups" are part of the learning process. The more practice he gets in a safe environment, the more likely he is to succeed.

In this example, Josh agrees that he wants to make a change. Mrs. Allgood shows him how to do it, and he gets a chance to practice during class. His awareness increases, and he receives ongoing support from Mrs. Allgood.

The post-it note strategy means that Josh is removing a negative. An alternative can be to add a positive. Mrs. Allgood gives him a pie chart, with eight slices. Each slice represents six minutes. Josh is told that every time six minutes goes by and he doesn't call out, he can shade in one of the slices. His goal is to have as many shaded slices as he can by the time the forty-eight minute class is over. He can use his watch or the wall clock. Younger kids can use a visual timer, where the red section grows smaller as the time counts down.

These strategies work best if Mrs. Allgood encourages Josh and speaks to him about what happens to him when he calls out. She can work with him one-on-one, modeling the things in class that distract him — which can be a lot of fun. Any way that she can get him to be aware of what he's choosing will help him speed up the desired changes.

Example 3. High school

Johnny has grown up. His name is now John. He is chronically late to his first period class. His tardies have piled up, his grade is slipping, but he still comes in late. Mrs. Allgood has a meeting with John to discuss his tardies. She asks, "Do you want your grade to keep going down?" As soon as he says, "No," she's accomplished number one — getting him to want to change.

This is the point where many teachers stop. They reason that the student wants to change, and the proof will be in the pudding. But Mrs. Allgood goes further. She talks with John about his pattern in the morning. He tells her that his alarm clock goes off on time, but he keeps hitting the snooze button. She suggests that he put the alarm clock on the other side of the room. She also suggests that John's classmate Susie call him in the morning to make sure he's up. John agrees to try. But Mrs. Allgood doesn't stop there. She knows that John is embarrassed about asking Susie, and may not actually do it. So she asks him when he will talk to her, and what he's going to say to get her to call him. She has John repeat the lines he needs to say. She then tells him that she'll check with Susie the next day to see how the process went. Only then does she end the conversation by encouraging him to succeed the next day.

Does John show up on time the next day? Maybe. He's certainly more likely to show up, now that he has admitted that he **wants to change,** he's looked at **how** to make that change, he's **practiced** what he needs to say, he's **aware** of his resistance and is willing to make the effort anyway, and he has **support** both from Mrs. Allgood and his friend Susie.

All teachers address one or more of these five steps with their students all the time. Putting them together into a more formal plan helps streamline the process, and helps fill in the gaps when students are still not changing their behavior.

How do I use these strategies with the limited time I have?

This process is labor intensive, and takes a lot of time and energy from the teacher. But it's worth it if we can help kids turn their behaviors around. One strategy is to start with the one student who adversely affects the rest of the class the most — usually it's the student whose absence gives us the biggest sigh of relief. Often if one or two key students stop misbehaving, the whole feeling in the class changes for the better.

What if my student doesn't want to change?

Most students will admit they want to change if we assume the best about them as we speak to them. We may have to wade through the noise in their heads ("I want ice cream and cake for dinner") to find what their gut is saying ("I need to eat vegetables").

We can frame the conversation in terms of power. Something students want is power and control in their lives. Calling out impulsively, for example, is a sign of a lack of power, a lack of self-control.

We can frame the conversation in terms of the practical: "Mark, do you really want to keep getting in trouble? I didn't think so…"

If a student still won't admit that he wants to change, we can assume it anyway: "Let's pretend for the time being that this does matter to you, and let's see what happens." It can still work.

Tips For Temporary Change

The above steps aren't always possible. Time is short, the student is reactive, and we are too focused elsewhere.

If this is the case, we can try other approaches described below. While they are not as thorough as those described above, they can help to lengthen the time between student misbehaviors.

Strategies

The conversation

A private conversation with a student after he has fulfilled his consequence can be a critical element in improving behavior. This

Mrs. Allgood says

> Start with the one student who adversely affects the rest of the class the most — usually it's the student whose absence gives us the biggest sigh of relief.

A Closer Look

> If a student still won't admit that he wants to change, we can assume it anyway. It can still work.

should be done after the "dust has settled," and he is receptive. We should address at least three things:

1. The student tells the teacher what his misbehavior was.
2. The student describes what appropriate behavior should look and sound like.
3. The teacher cleans the slate, creating or reestablishing a positive connection with the student, welcoming him back into the classroom community.

This follow-up conversation can be quick, and while not a guarantee that change will stick, it often can make a huge difference in disarming chronic student misbehavior. It helps the student look squarely at the choices he was making and can make in the future, and it helps him remember that the teacher is on his side. If time is too short for all three steps, the teacher can do the talking in steps one and two, telling the student what his behavior was and what it should be in the future. The most important of the three steps is number three. The positive connection between student and teacher is often what it takes to short-circuit chronic student misbehavior. A combination of firm (using consequences) and soft (nurturing a positive connection) is often enough to help kids turn their behavior around.

Our skill at this type of conversation will grow over time. Our interpersonal skills come sharply into focus, as we wend our way in to our students' hearts, skirting around and under their defenses, and reminding them that not only are they responsible, they are also respected and welcome.

Mrs. Allgood says

> Our skill at this type of conversation will grow over time. Our interpersonal skills come sharply into focus, as we wend our way in to our students' hearts.

Use writing

One option is to have students fill out a form when they are serving a time-out or a visit to the office. The form can ask them several key questions, such as:

▲ What happened?

▲ How did you feel?

▲ What did you do?

▲ What are you going to do next time?

A Closer Look

The positive connection between student and teacher is often what it takes to short-circuit chronic student misbehavior.

Another writing option is a student-generated action plan for changing behavior. Questions can include:

▲ What do you need to change?

▲ What's the cause?

▲ What's your solution, and what are the steps involved?

▲ How will you practice those steps?

▲ What type of support do you need?

▲ How will you keep track of your own progress?

▲ How will you know when the problem has been solved?

These forms won't necessarily end conflict, but they will allow the student some reflection time where he can slow down and be more prepared to squarely and positively address his behavior.

Behavior contracts

Teachers can create individual behavior contracts for students, focused on changing one student behavior at a time. The contracts should be signed by the student, his parents, and the teacher. They can be as behavioral and nit-picky as we want. The focus is to break appropriate behaviors into smaller, doable parts, and to monitor and build upon the successes he shows. Tying success on the contract to privileges at home works well. Tying it to school privileges is also effective. Behavior contracts are particularly successful if the students have a hand in designing them, and if they include a timeline and/or rubric for students to monitor their progress.

A Closer Look

Behavior contracts should ideally be focused on one behavior at a time.

Wise Apple Advice

A last word on breaking the cycle

The common threads among all the approaches in this chapter are simple:

▲ Make positive connections with students
▲ Assume the best — the students want to make a change
▲ Break the change into simpler and simpler steps
▲ Give students a chance to reflect on their choices
▲ Provide students the chance to take responsibility for their choices
▲ Check progress as we go, and provide support along the way

Not coincidentally, these approaches are the same whether we are teaching content, procedures, or behavior. Once we internalize the pattern of these approaches, there is no limit to the creative solutions that we can discover in working with our students.

14

PUTTING IT ALL TOGETHER — FINAL THOUGHTS

> "To learn and never be filled —
> is wisdom.
> To teach and never be weary —
> is love."
>
> — AUTHOR UNKNOWN

Classroom Management: The Big Picture

We've looked at effective classroom management from a variety of perspectives. By examining Mrs. Meanswell's attempts and Mrs. Allgood's successes, we've illuminated critical ideas and techniques that are normally invisible. Below is the same diagram that we started with, showing these keys:

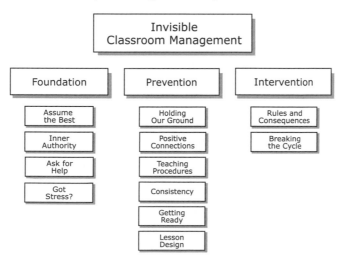

Effective classroom management isn't simply a matter of doling out consequences, connecting positively with students, or designing great lessons. There is no one magic approach — but a variety of them.

When I observe a teacher's classroom in search of classroom management skills, I look for many guideposts, which I've compiled in the checklist that follows. Although there are no clear-cut "rights" and "wrongs" in the checklist, its components can act as specific reminders, or can combine to provide a broad perspective.

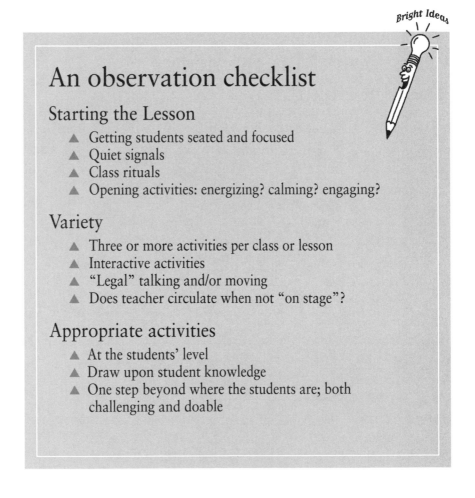

Bright Ideas

An observation checklist

Starting the Lesson

- ▲ Getting students seated and focused
- ▲ Quiet signals
- ▲ Class rituals
- ▲ Opening activities: energizing? calming? engaging?

Variety

- ▲ Three or more activities per class or lesson
- ▲ Interactive activities
- ▲ "Legal" talking and/or moving
- ▲ Does teacher circulate when not "on stage"?

Appropriate activities

- ▲ At the students' level
- ▲ Draw upon student knowledge
- ▲ One step beyond where the students are; both challenging and doable

Student involvement

- ▲ How does the teacher include all students during a lesson or discussion?
- ▲ How are groups set up and maintained?
- ▲ How does the teacher focus on student responsibility and accountability?
- ▲ How efficient is the teacher's use of time?

Clear procedures

- ▲ Are procedures taught? How?
- ▲ Are they practiced? How?
- ▲ How are they reinforced and maintained?
- ▲ Does the teacher check for understanding?
- ▲ Which procedures are used for transitions?
- ▲ What procedures work well?
- ▲ How were they taught and implemented over time?

Consistency

- ▲ Students raising hands
- ▲ Teacher staying focused on topic, deflecting distractions
- ▲ All students are engaged before teacher speaks with individual students
- ▲ All students are treated equally with dignity and respect

Keeping students focused

- ▲ Teacher proximity
- ▲ Teacher posture
- ▲ Teacher tone and volume
- ▲ Teacher efficiency when circulating to help students

Behavior/consequences

- ▲ Are rules and consequences clear to the teacher? To the students?
- ▲ Are rules essential or extraneous?
- ▲ Do consequences fit the behaviors?
- ▲ Are they consistently and fairly enforced?

Holding ground

- ▲ What is the quality of the teacher's "no"?
- ▲ Is the teacher assuming the best of herself and her students?
- ▲ Is the enforcement of consequences easy or labored? Does the teacher have public arguments, or private discussions?
- ▲ Is there a sense of mutual respect?
- ▲ A level of relaxation and simultaneous authority?

Positive reinforcement

- ▲ Do the students feel recognized and appreciated?
- ▲ Does the teacher smile?
- ▲ Is the teacher enthusiastic? Energizing? Warm?
- ▲ Does she encourage students?
- ▲ Is the class fun? Funny? Interesting? Exciting?
- ▲ Is there a sense of a joy of learning and teaching?

Architecture

- ▲ Students' proximity and access to the teacher, to each other, and to materials
- ▲ Smooth flow of traffic
- ▲ Wall decorations
- ▲ Overall feel of the environment: prison or playground?

Closure

- ▲ What culminating/reflective activities take place?
- ▲ Does the class look at the big picture?

Teaching and Learning: The Big Picture

A Closer Look

There is something fundamental and beautiful — wonder — underlying all the details of teaching.

Several years ago I observed a beginning science teacher and saw a fabulous lesson. Light bulbs were going off in kids' heads all over the classroom. It was truly inspiring. When I went to document what I saw, I found that the education standards forms I had were inadequate to do justice to what I was seeing in the classroom. I realized then that there is more to learning than jumping through the hoops that we're taught in credential school. True learning involves several connected experiences and choices, as described in the "recipe" below

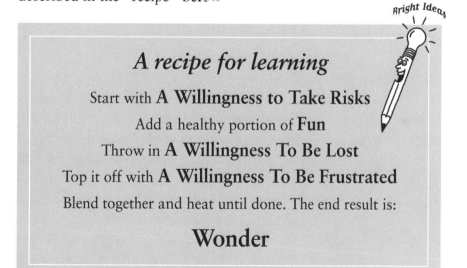

Bright Ideas

A recipe for learning

Start with **A Willingness to Take Risks**

Add a healthy portion of **Fun**

Throw in **A Willingness To Be Lost**

Top it off with **A Willingness To Be Frustrated**

Blend together and heat until done. The end result is:

Wonder

Let's "unpack" this recipe one ingredient at a time.

A willingness to take risks

Just as in the old "Star Trek" series, we can't beam people onto the ship if our shields are up. Risking means lowering our guard, thereby opening ourselves up to new experiences and new learning. Chapter 4, "Asking for Help," addressed this quality of openness in detail.

A healthy portion of fun

True learning is exhilarating, breathtaking, mind expanding, and fun. With all the testing, grades, and homework, we often seem to lose our connection to this. For a visceral reminder of learning and fun, try observing a child learning to read or shooting a basket for the first time.

A willingness to be lost

The moment before we learn something, we don't yet know it. We are lost. If we push away the experience of "lostness," we won't stick around long enough to receive the knowledge that lies there, waiting.

A willingness to be frustrated

Several years ago, I designed a lesson where pairs of students shared computers and used a new geography software program to find the answers on a worksheet. I gave the students only half a minute of instruction as to how to navigate through the program, knowing that it would force them to explore on their own. Sure enough, two types of students emerged. Mark pushed his chair away from the computer in frustration, saying, "This is dumb. I hate doing this." Maria, on the other hand, got totally into it, saying, "This is cool. It's like looking for buried treasure, using the computer mouse as a flashlight." Mark felt frustration and pushed it away. Maria embraced frustration and was propelled forward into learning and wonder.

> True learning is exhilarating, breathtaking, mind expanding, and fun.

By combining these four ingredients, we reveal a sense of wonder, the magic that is at the heart of true learning. I include this recipe as a reminder that there is something fundamental and beautiful — wonder — underlying all the details of teaching. It is one of the reasons many of us got into the profession. By consciously searching for, facilitating, and promoting these four ingredients, we can help increase the moments of wonder in our classrooms.

Further, the two points of view illustrated by Mark and Maria are the two polarities that we are faced with every day with students in the classroom, and every moment of our own lives. Do we let frustration get the best of us? Or do we step through it into wonder? Do we buy into the waves of noise in our heads? Or do we honor what we know in our hearts and in our guts? As we facilitate ways for our students to navigate through these waters, we provide ourselves the same skills. The reverse is also true. As we grow in our own self-appreciation and wonder, we naturally find ways to help our students do the same.

A Closer Look

As we facilitate ways for our students to navigate through these waters, we provide ourselves the same skills.

Our Own Lives: The *Really* Big Picture

In Chapter 6, "Holding our Ground," we covered a fundamental concept that has implications reaching far beyond the classroom. An extension of the frustrating-technology example, this concept addressed recognizing our feelings, of anger, for example, without reacting to them. Our ability to be truly happy is, I believe, tied directly to the notion that real happiness is a choice we can make regardless of the transitory experiences we are feeling.

As teachers we choose to take care of business even when we feel angry or guilty. As human beings we can choose to take care of ourselves, our loved ones, and the earth in the same way, by recognizing but not indulging our experiences. The truly visionary leaders in the world are those who can do this on a large scale — receiving and welcoming all their feelings as they stay relaxed and yet passionate about their beliefs. This requires a deep commitment to assuming the best about ourselves and others, even in the light of all the evidence we could use to support the contrary. All human beings have the capacity for goodness. The challenge is to access that in ourselves as we access it in others. The arena of classroom management is overflowing with opportunity to embrace this. What more challenging environment can there be to continue to assume and remember the best about people?

▲ ▲ ▲

A second, related concept was discussed in Chapter 3, "Inner Authority," and addressed the continuum of inner apology and inner authority. This internal muscle grows over time as we focus on holding our ground, not over-explaining, teaching procedures, being consistent, and delivering consequences in a soft and firm manner. There is, I believe, no limit to how much the muscle can grow, and no area in life where this muscle isn't present. Whether it's getting students to put their things away, getting a friend to help us out, holding our ground with our son or daughter, communicating our political agenda in a room full of adversaries, expressing our deep love for a friend or for the earth, or stopping tanks in their tracks — all involve this muscle of inner authority.

As we continually reflect on our level of self-apology, bringing to consciousness our resistances to self-expression, we get a chance to blossom and grow in self-regard, courage, and confidence. The continuum is infinite. It is, I believe, the single defining characteristic of greatness in this world — one's willingness to stand up and hold one's ground with the noise in one's head, and the people in one's world, while assuming the best, in ways that invite cooperation. People like Gandhi and Martin Luther King, Jr., come to mind. They had the power of their convictions, their love of self and other, to hold firmly to what they believed, even in the face of tremendous resistance. Ultimately they were able to melt much of

A Closer Look

Real happiness is a choice we can make regardless of the transitory experiences we are feeling.

A Closer Look

The muscle that allows us to successfully manage our classrooms is the same muscle that allows us to move mountains in the world.

that resistance, because of the strength that they had discovered inside themselves, and because of their willingness to assume the best even about the very people who seemingly stood in their way.

Even though these actions seem so different, the muscle that allows us to successfully manage our classrooms is the same muscle that allows us to move mountains in the world. Finding ways to hold our ground in the classroom while still caring for our students is good practice for succeeding and enjoying all aspects of our lives, and for extending our influence beyond the classroom or school into the world at large.

*"There are two things
we must give children:
The first one is roots,
the other, wings."*

— AUTHOR UNKNOWN

INDEX

Absent students 119, 143-144

Action thermometer 129-130, 156

Active listening 203

ADHD strategy 204

ADOPT system for documentation 191-192

Anger

    - student 25, 76

    - teacher 60-62, 184-185, 221

Apology 23-26, 63, 96, 101, 222

Appreciation vs praise 197

Arguing with the ref 108, 166

Assessment 136, 137, 151

Bathroom procedure 103

Before-School-Checklist 116-122, 131

Behavior contracts 179, 212

Bias 155

Big Lie, the 128

Blurting - (see "calling out")

Breathing 47, 156

Calling out 192, 204, 207, 208

Card system for documentation 192

Caring 24, 33, 48-49, 59, 65-66, 111-112, 223

Changing your system 193-194

Chaos to end class 187

Characteristics of a good teacher 32

Charge transfer game 78

Check for understanding 86, 101, 141-143, 157-159

Checklist for management 216-218

Choice and responsibility 12, 14, 69-71, 167, 171-173,

180-181, 187, 205-210

Choral recital 149

Clean slate 151

Closure 135-137, 157-159, 218

Complaints from students 94

Consequences 162-199

   - choosing consequences 190

   - examples 173, 175-179

   - natural/logical 173

   - provide wiggle room for teacher 173

   - specific and concrete 174, 176

   - student participation in 180

Coupons for behavior 98

Cross-laterals 156

Dan and the flying hammer 168-170

Directions

   - clarity 82, 100-102

   - for group work 86-90, 102

   - (see also "check for understanding")

Document everything 39

Down-time for teachers 153

Emotional Intelligence 12, 154

Emotions 49, 62

   - charge transfer game 78

Evaluations, understanding and sharing 38-39

Explaining our reasons 57-59

Extrinsic vs intrinsic motivation 163, 196-198

Eye contact 96

Filler 152-153

Finishing early 138, 151-152

Firm and soft paradox 7, 22, 29, 56, 167, 172, 178

First things to do 131

Five minutes a day 47-48

Five step lesson plan 135-137

Framing a lesson 140

Frisbee throw 157

Frustration 141, 154, 202, 219-220

Fun 13, 141, 208, 218, 219-220

Gandhi 222

Grading 120, 137, 147

   - vs. feedback 151

Group incentives 97, 195

Group work 86-90, 102

Guilt 60, 62, 221

Hand raising 106-108, 166

Hand signals 99-100

Head, heart, and gut 67

Help synonyms 36

Hired last minute 124

Homework 136, 158-159

Implementing changes 193-194

Independent work 136-137, 186, 187

Infinite job description 45

Interviews between students 128

Invisible classroom management 4

Invisible contract 13-15

I-statements 203

Jokes and laughter 94

Late work 144

Lawyers, students as 105, 110

Logbook for assignments 143, 144

Martin Luther King, Jr. 222

Metaphors to help retention 158

Mistakes by the teacher 23, 31, 33

Multi-cultural education 155

Music for transitions 98

Musical chairs 130

Names

    - contests 130

    - using student names 96

Nice vs. kind 66

No 57, 59, 60

Office, sending students 178

Openness is win-win 37

P.E. teachers 21, 185, 190-191

Parents/guardians 29, 179

People hunt 127, 129

Personal connections

    - too far? 73, 74

    - writing 73

Phil the baiter 16

Please 101

Popcorn effect 110

Positive connections 64-79, 203, 211-213

Post-it notes 126, 175, 207-208

Posture 56
Praise 186, 197
Principles 164
Procedures 80-103
    - list of classroom procedures 83-85
    - precede content 88
    - railroad tracks 82
    - rubrics for procedures 92
    - two per class or lesson 90-92
Proximity 95
Quizzes on rules 129, 182
Racism 155
Reactivity 60-63
Recipe for learning 219
Reciprocal teaching 157
Reflection 28
Rewards and gifts 196-198
Risk-taking 31, 32, 219
Role models 41
Room arrangement 92, 118, 125-126
Rules 165-167
Saving face 174, 189
Seating arrangement – (see "room arrangement")
Self-evaluation from the future 129
Silence before talking 98
Silent work to start a lesson 138
Slow down delivery 148
Sound signals 99
Starting class, students entering 93, 96

Stress. 42-52
        - airplane analogy 44-46, 48
        - biggest source 43-44
        - December holidays 51
Stretching 156
Talking, legal 146-147
Tardies 208-209
Tattling 95
Test, when kids test us 14-15
Timer 97, 175, 187, 198, 208
Transferring students 39
Transitions 198, 205, 217
        - changing student behavior 205, 206
        - consistency 105
        - music for 98
        - using a timer 97
Treasure hunt. 127, 147
Variety in lessons 146, 216
Voice, volume, tone 56, 96, 185
Wait time 133, 148
What to do first 131
Why students act out 14-16, 202
Wonder 219-220
Writing
        - behavior contracts 179, 212
        - for documentation 39
        - for personal connections 73
        - to teach behavior 211, 212

Praise for Rick Smith's
Conscious Classroom Management
Seminars

"Wow! This is going to be wonderfully helpful information! I can't wait to start implementing! I am feeling incredibly charged and energized! Thank you!"
— Jen B., 3rd Grade

"I've taught for 22 years. I've been to several seminars and workshops over those years. This was by far the very best workshop I've attended. I feel ready for this semester! Thank you! Thank you! Thank you!"
— Leslie B., Middle School

"I am anxious to return to the classroom after taking Rick's workshop. I believe that I can be a better teacher and have more fun doing it."
— Robert B., Middle School

"Fantastic! So much <u>stuff I could use</u> I ran out of time to write! Loved the fact that you gave examples for use in all grades. I would attend any workshops you gave here! Thanks <u>so much!</u>"
— Erica M., 1st Grade

"Wow! You articulate things I haven't even thought of sharing with my beginning teachers. Thanks!"
— George P., Mentor Teacher

"This was the most useful workshop I have been to. I got more ideas for the problems I am experiencing than all the workshops I have been to combined. I really enjoyed the interactive part and the humor you brought to the presentation. You're an excellent presenter and provide a great service to teachers."
— Christie M., High School

"Super loaded with <u>useful</u> strategies. High energy – should be sent to <u>all</u> schools in the district – to ensure his knowledge is passed on."
— Michele N., 6th Grade

"You gave me some wonderful, helpful ideas I can share immediately, and over time. After 27 years you've helped me learn more!"
– Cara K.,
Elementary Principal

"No other workshop has given me as many tools to take back to the classroom and implement instantly. Thank you!!"
– Samantha A., 1st Grade

"This was probably the best workshop I have ever participated in. Informative, useful, and based on research. The presenter is knowledgable and entertaining – a very powerful combination."
– Barbara C.,
Mentor Teacher

"This was the best workshop I've attended ever. There are so many concrete ideas, my difficulty will be which one will I implement first!"
– Brenda H.,
High School English

"Best workshop I've been to. "Real" practical ideas and strategies delivered with humor and professionalism. Validated all emotions of (struggling) teachers. Very positive and motivating. Great analogies and metaphors. Kept my interest all day! Rick is fabulous!"
– Susan W., 6th Grade

"I am saying this in all honesty that this is the best workshop I have been to! I will use so many things. I really enjoy your approach with the music, Frisbees, and juggling. You were fantastic. Thank you!"
– Jennifer G., 3rd Grade

"This was hands-down the best class or workshop that I have ever attended."
– Erica R., 3rd Grade

"Rick put into action what he was teaching us. Fabulous role model! Great workshop!"
– Karen W., 5th Grade

"I feel more equipped to have a happier, more productive classroom and year... I found the workshop to be great."
— Laura M.,
Middle School Spanish

"This was the most useful workshop I've ever attended. Your handout will be referred to often."
— Mike G., Middle School

"Best workshop I have attended! I've probably been to 10-12 in the past several years, on a wide range of topics, and this workshop was superior!"
— Paul K.,
High School English

"Such a fast paced workshop – virtually no wasted time – wonderful, practical ideas."
— Kathy A., 4th grade

"Rick has super energy and has so much to share. Please have Rick talk to all the teachers in our district!!! You give inspiration to our profession."
— Laura T., Mentor Teacher

"I found your class to be inspiring. I feel guilty how I have been teaching... I am sure glad I have some new strategies to take back so I won't get burnt out by the end of the year. Only class I have enjoyed!"
— Erin P. 4th grade

"Realistic scenarios, timely injections of humor; sensitivity to various levels/grades. Very valuable/useful presentation!!"
— Anon Middle School

"Rick is a wonder. I am taking so much back with me to share. This is the best I've heard in many years."
— Maria V., Mentor Teacher

235

Notes

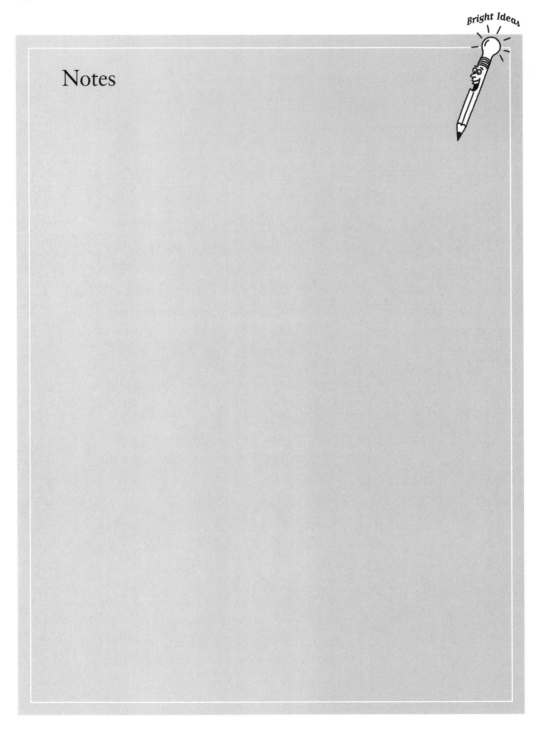

Notes

Notes

Bright Ideas

Bright Ideas

Notes

Rick Smith is an award winning teacher, education consultant and international presenter. He taught students in San Rafael, CA for over fifteen years (with a primary focus on students at-risk), and was a mentor/support provider and mentor coordinator for seven years. He has taught in the Secondary Credential Program at Dominican College in San Rafael, CA and has trained American Peace Corps Volunteer Teachers in Ghana, West Africa. Rick's  Masters thesis, entitled "Mentoring New Teachers: Strategies, Structures, and Successes," appears in Teacher Education Quarterly, Autumn, 1993. His article "Assume the Best for Student Success" appears in ASCD's Classroom Leadership, October 2002. He has given numerous keynotes, pre-conference and concurrent sessions at state and national conferences throughout the United States. Currently, he teaches part-time in the Elementary Credential Program at St. Mary's College in Moraga, CA and mentors beginning teachers in the San Francisco Bay Area.

Rick's workshops include:

▲ *Conscious Classroom Management: Bringing Out The Best in Students and Teachers*

▲ *Rebels With Applause: Brain Compatible Approaches For Motivating Reluctant Learners*

▲ *Nuts and Bolts for Mentor Teachers: Strategies that Make a Difference*

▲ *Brain Compatible Presentation Skills for Teachers and Teacher-Trainers*

Rick's goal is to bring out the best in students and teachers, by offering nurturing ways to bring fun and challenge to education, and by giving teachers tools for surfing the challenging waves of the classroom experience.

To contact Rick about workshops,
or to purchase books, please contact him at:

Rick Smith – Conscious Teaching
21 Crest Road
Fairfax, California 94930
ricksmith@consciousteaching.com
www.consciousteaching.com
1-800-667-6062